OPERATION JAPAN

JAPAN in focus

a handbook for PRAYER

Operation Japan Publishing Committee
and
Japan Evangelical Missionary Association

Operation Japan Publishing Committee
Author and Committee Chairman: Haruo Mitsumori

English Editor: Don Wright
Printer: New Life Mission, Japan
Co-Publisher: Japan Evangelical Missionary Association
C/O OCC Bldg., 2-1 Kanda Surugadai
Chiyoda Ku, Tokyo 101, Japan
Tel/Fax: 03-3295-1949

Printed in Japan
ISBN4-9900576-2-7

Cover Design: Michael Smith

Contents

Locating Topics

Prayer Notes

Explaining the Book

The Author: Rev. Haruo Mitsumori was born in Tokyo in 1929, is married with five children and one grandchild, and pastors the Immanuel Oji Church in Tokyo area. He has served in many capacities within the evangelical church of Japan, and has written seven books. Presently he serves as board chairman of Church Information Service.

We offer you this first English edition of *Operation Japan* as a prayer tool for Japan. We thank God for the many people around the world who have prayed for this country over the years. However, often the information available has been very limited, causing many of us to pray, "Lord, bless Japan. Lord, save Japan." In this little book Rev. Haruo Mitsumori and others have given us an abundance of material to target Japan for Jesus in a new way.

As you pray, please remember the following:

1. Japan is a non-Christian nation with about four out of a thousand who are members of a Protestant church. Less than half of these members attend a church, and when you include the seekers, there are only 2.1 people in a thousand who attend a worship service. In this context at times the Lord uses things that may seem only indirectly related to the gospel, for example, the Bible being mentioned in a secular novel, a couple being married in a Western "Christian" wedding, children attending a Catholic school, or even studying the Bible with a Jehovah's Witness.

2. Not all of the institutions listed in the prayer requests are evangelical. Some started out as Christian, but perhaps now have only a remnant of influence remaining. We have decided to ask you to pray for these, because the name of Jesus is represented in some way. Our prayer is that the Lord will create an interest in the gospel which will lead people to a saving knowledge of Jesus.

3. As you pray for the Christian book stores, remember that these are not only serving Christians, but are also evangelistic outposts. The radio and TV broadcasts encourage believers, and have a powerful evangelistic potential as well. Church kindergartens or hospitals can provide major first steps toward Jesus. Also remember that a large majority of students in all levels of Christian schools (except Bible schools and seminaries) are not Christians. These also are evangelistic opportunities.

4. Japanese Christians need much encouragement to be faithful since they are such a small minority. There are many family and cultural pressures to conform in this group-oriented society, making it difficult to stand up for their faith. When we ask you to pray for the fellowship and cooperation of churches and Christians in each prefecture, remember that this is a very important request.

Don Wright, English Editor
Baptist General Conference Missionary

北海道 Hokkaido

Capital: Sapporo
Population: 5,684,842
Cities: 32
  With 0 churches: 2
  With 1 church: 3
Towns/Villages: 180
  With no churches: 117
  With 20,000 pop. & no churches: 4

Size: 83,519 km^2
Density: 68 people/km^2
Churches: P 391, C 70
Church per pop.: 1:14,539
Worship attendance: 10,743
Attendance/church: 27
Missionaries: 140

Explanation of Statistics Box:

Churches: P 391 *(Protestant churches) From CIS report, 1996*
          C 70 (Catholic churches) *From Christian Year Book, 1997*
Church per pop.: 1:14,539 *One church for every 14,539 people*
Worship attendance: 10,743 *Total worship attendance of the Protestant churches*
Attendance/church: 27 *Average attendance per Protestant church*
Missionaries: 140 *Number of Protestant missionaries, JEMA Directory 1997*
Attendance/pop.: 0.15 *In the district statistics we have included this category,*
    meaning 1.5 people attending Protestant churches for every 1,000 people

Word Guide:

CIS	Church Information Service
CLC	Christian Literature Crusade
JEA	Japan Evangelical Association
JEMA	Japan Evangelical Missionary Association
Kirishitan	Catholic believers in the late 1500s until the beginning of the Meiji era

Pronunciation

You do not need to pronounce the names correctly for the Lord to understand!
However, if you would like to try, the following will help for the vowels:
Whenever you see: "a," pronounce it as the "a" in ball.
               "i," pronounce it as the "ea" of eat.
               "u," pronounce it as the "oo" of boot.
               "e," pronounce it as the "e" of end.
               "o," pronounce it as the "oa" of oar.
In Japanese some vowels are lengthened. An example would be the lengthened "o" is written either as "ou," "oo" or o-. For simplification, we have chosen not to include any lengthened vowel indicators.

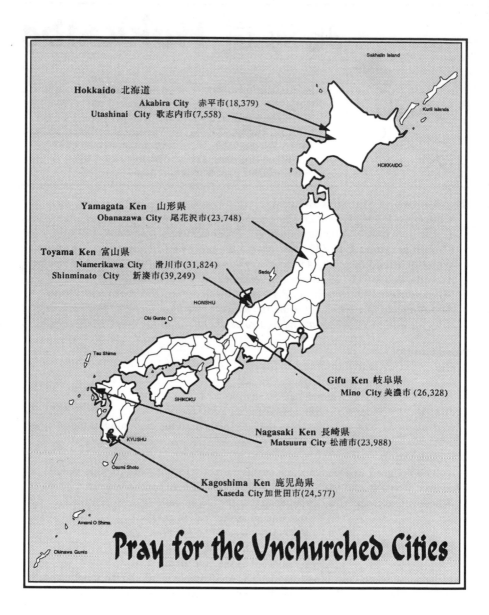

Hokkaido 北海道
Akabira City　赤平市(18,379)
Utashinai City 歌志内市(7,558)

Yamagata Ken　山形県
Obanazawa City　尾花沢市(23,748)

Toyama Ken 富山県
Namerikawa City　滑川市(31,824)
Shinminato City　新湊市(39,249)

Gifu Ken 岐阜県
Mino City 美濃市 (26,328)

Nagasaki Ken 長崎県
Matsuura City 松浦市(23,988)

Kagoshima Ken 鹿児島県
Kaseda City 加世田市(24,577)

Pray for the Unchurched Cities

Churches Around the World

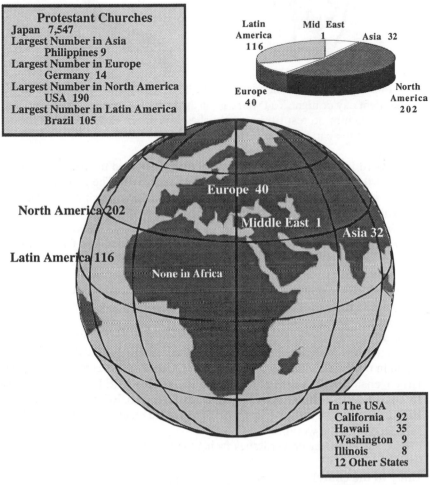

Protestant Churches
Japan 7,547
Largest Number in Asia
  Philippines 9
Largest Number in Europe
  Germany 14
Largest Number in North America
  USA 190
Largest Number in Latin America
  Brazil 105

Latin America 116
Mid East 1
Asia 32
Europe 40
North America 202

North America 202

Latin America 116

Europe 40

Middle East 1

Asia 32

None in Africa

In The USA
  California   92
  Hawaii   35
  Washington 9
  Illinois   8
  12 Other States

Statistics taken from *The Japan Christian Year Book* (1996)
First printed in JEA *Japan Update*, Fall 1996

9

Prayer for Japan

I have posted watchmen on your walls, O Jerusalem; they will never be silent day or night. You who call on the Lord, give yourselves no rest, and give him no rest till he establishes Jerusalem and makes her the praise of the earth (Isaiah 62:6,7).

The Lord is raising up intercessors all over the world to spearhead the advance of the church into unreached and resistant areas. The fact that you are reading this article indicates that the Lord is establishing watchmen on the walls to petition the Lord for His people in Japan. You are part of a growing stream that will ultimately turn into a river of revival for the nation of Japan. This prayer guide is being used around the world to link Japanese Christians and Japan watchers in a prayer-net of intercession.

You have an extremely important position in Kingdom work. Do not grow weary in well doing through prayer. Carve out time for prayer. We consider this guide not so much as a finished product that includes all the needs of Japan and the church, but rather as an introduction and starting point for prayer As you focus your heart on Japan, ask the Lord to broaden your heart with the deep things that are on His heart for His people in Japan. Along with the requests found in the guide, ask Him for things that reflect His character, His glory and His covenant love for His people. YOUR PRAYERS ARE FOUNDATIONAL IN BRINGING SPIRITUAL CHANGE TO THE CHURCH!! Therefore ASK BIG; base your prayers on His greatness. May He enlarge your heart for Himself, Japan and the world..

Here are some key prayer issues facing the church in Japan.

Unity in the church

The church is split into over 120 denominations. There are major divisions between Charismatic, Evangelical and Mainline churches with little communication or cooperation between them. Pray that these barriers will be broken down and a spirit of John 17:21 lived out.

Leadership training

Pastors, though trained in theology, need to have a vision for and the skill to train dedicated disciples. Another concern is that even though the church has been growing at a very slow rate, because of low seminary enrollment and retirements there will be a major shortage of pastors by the year 2010. Ask the Lord to provide such people as described in II Timothy 2:2 and I Timothy 3:1 for the church in Japan.

Discipleship

Application of biblical truth on a daily basis is a great challenge for believers who are continually being pressured to conform to this monolithic, homogeneous culture. This keeps many Christians from a consistent witness and worship. Many baptized Japanese fall away within the first five years. Ask the Lord to impart a grace to His people that will enable them to live out Romans 12:2-20.

Intercession

Since revival is preceded by a spirit of prayer and intercession, people, with a God-granted burden to labor in prayer are greatly needed. Ask the Lord to establish more and more watchmen (Isaiah 62:6,7).

Revitalized worship

Many of the conservative churches maintain a form-centered worship that lacks the vitality of the Spirit. Ask the Lord to break in and give His people a new song to sing for the praise of His name (Psalm 98).

Missions

The Japanese church has only begun to be a blessing to the nations. Ask the Lord to grant a vision and burden for the nations of the earth to His church. Japan is remembered among the Asian people as the nation that caused great harm and hurt during World War II. Ask the Lord to make the church a balm and blessing to the nations of Asia (Isaiah 49:6).

May the Lord strengthen your heart and make you a blessing to Japan and all nations through prayer.

Dave Walker
OC International Missionary

11

Trends and Issues

1. Rise and fall of religious cults

In the past ten years or more Japan has seen a rise in the number of "New Religion" cults especially attracting Japanese young people (college through young career age). A common draw is the promise of inner fulfillment through a variety of techniques of meditation, yoga, mind control and asceticism. In 1995 the exposure of the Supreme Truth (AUM) cult behind the sarin gas attacks on the Tokyo subway and other parts of Japan shocked the nation. Mind control methods used by the cults have received wide attention from the media. This is an opportunity for the church to declare the Truth of God's Word.

2. Scandalous politics

It seems that every month for the past five or six years a new scandal has been revealed among Japan's business and government leaders. A basic lack of interest in politics, coupled with complacency toward the democratic system, has allowed abuses in government. Kickbacks and payoffs constitute the majority of these scandals. And yet there is very little outcry from the ordinary citizen. Two celebrities won mayoral positions in Japan's two largest cities, Tokyo and Osaka, because of their position on clean government. Christian voices are seldom raised on political issues.

3. De-urbanization

Tokyo and Osaka are experiencing a drop in population as city-dwellers flee to the countryside for better living conditions. Commuting two hours one way to work has become the norm. Huge bedroom towns in the outlying areas of major cities are virtually vacant during the day. New approaches in evangelism are necessary to reach these communities with the gospel.

4. Revival movement

In 1996 over 500 individual churches and pastors throughout Japan joined a new association of Christian churches with the purpose of encouraging revival. Some church leaders are concerned that this indicates another division in an already fragmented, frail church. There is frustration with the ineffectiveness of the church to bring change in Japan.

5. Lay leadership training

Most seminaries and Bible schools are experiencing a decrease in student enrollment. However, Bible schools open to laypeople are experiencing record enrollments. Ochanomizu Bible Institute reports over 100 students enrolled each year. Japan To Jesus (JTJ) offers Bible school training by correspondence. Hundreds are enrolled each year here also.

6. Aging society

The "graying of Japan" is becoming a concern along with a projected decrease of the Japanese work force. Nursing homes have long waiting lists. The demise of the two and three generation household has begun as young families put their elderly in retirement and nursing homes. King's Garden nursing homes, a Christian ministry to the elderly, has met with great success with a dozen centers being built throughout Japan. Although partially funded by the government, the nursing homes are still free to hold daily chapels and share the gospel with residents, many of whom receive new hope in Christ.

7. Lack of moral values among youth

Matter-of-fact reports in national newspapers of junior and senior high school girls selling their virginity to businessmen for $500 to $1000 continue to alarm parent groups. Church Information Service continues to report declines in church school attendance among evangelical churches throughout Japan. Churches find it difficult to hold the youth once they have entered junior high. One evangelical university professor declared that the state of the youth is an indicator of the ineffectiveness of the Church's message.

Ron Sisco, President
Japan Evangelical Missionary
Association (JEMA)
OC International Missionary

Japan History

8000 BC - cir. 250 AD Jomon Culture

Hunting and gathering. Yayoi people introduce rice cultivation, weaving, iron tools, horses and cattle.

cir. 250 -710 Yamato Period

A new culture appears. Rulers emerge claiming descent from sun goddess Amaterasu who is esteemed as the highest Shinto deity. Buddhism introduced from Korea. Chinese political theory of centralized imperial government introduced. Land claimed by the emperor. Taxation, civil and penal laws initiated. Chinese script adopted.

710 - 794 Nara Period

First permanent capital in Nara in 710. Transformation from tribal to aristocratic culture. Buddhism is linked to aristocracy and becomes a major force.

794 - 1180   Heian and the Fujiwaras

Emperor Kammu establishes imperial independence by locating capital in Heian (modern Kyoto). Fujiwara family rises to power through intermarriage with imperial family, assigning themselves as regent to the emperor. New Buddhist sects emerge in Heian ending the Nara Buddhist monopoly. Land falls into private aristocratic and religious ownership. Emergence of the rural Samurai warrior class.

1180 - 1192 The Beginning of Shogunates

Minamoto family defeats Taira family in the Gempei War to become the first national military rulers.

1192 - 1338 Kamakura Period

A period of power struggle between the imperial and shogunal lines of authority. Two Mongol invasions repelled by warriors assisted by storms described as divine winds (*kamikaze*). A time of "spiritual awakening." Buddhism is simplified — new sects introduced that guarantee salvation to all believers. In 1334, emperor Go-Daigo reasserts imperial authority (the Kemmu Restoration) resulting in two rival imperial courts.

1338 - 1560 Ashikaga Period

Ashikaga family reaches height of power under third shogun, ending the imperial schism. The shogunate rests on an alliance with local military leaders. Onin War effectively destroys Ashikaga authority and begins 100 years of wars, resulting in the rise of local feudal lords. Portuguese begin trade in 1545; Francis Xavier, the first Jesuit missionary, introduces Catholicism in 1549.

1560 - 1600 Period of Unification

Japan is reunified by a succession of three great feudal lords.

1600 - 1867 Tokugawa Period

From their castle city of Edo (modern Tokyo) the Tokugawas rule Japan. Key cities and mines are controlled by vassal lords, relatives and other subservient lords. After 1639 the nation enters seclusion. Nagasaki is only point of contact with foreign countries. By 19th century the old socioeconomic system virtually collapses. U.S. Commodore Perry forces Japan to abandon seclusionist policy in 1854. Tokugawa's leadership is questioned by feudal lords. In 1867 - 1868 the shogun is forced to resign, and imperial government is restored under Emperor Meiji.

1868 - 1912 Meiji Period

Japan is transformed from a secluded feudal society into an industrialized world power. 1873 — feudal land system abolished, tax system introduced; 1872 — centralized school system; 1889 — constitutional monarchy in place (emperor regarded as divine figure); 1894-95 — Sino-Japanese War, Korea conquered. 1904-5 — Russo-Japanese War, Sakhalin added to Japanese empire.

1912 - 1941 WWI and interwar years

Japan enters WWI as ally of Britain and seizes several German holdings in East Asia including Kiaochow, China. Japan's influence in China is extended. Postwar naval treaties are signed with West. Japanese military and government disagree with each other over expansionist issues. Fueled by the World Depression of the 30s, militarists rally public support. Terrorist groups assassinate 3 of 11 prime ministers. In 1931, military officers lead the occupation of Manchuria without government authorization. Three months after the establishment of the Manchukuo puppet state in Feb. 1932, military and civilian bureaucrats take over control of Japan national government. By 1940, after a second Sino-Japanese war, Japan controls eastern China from a puppet regime in Nanking. Japan allies with Axis powers already at war in Europe. Japanese troops occupy northern French Indochina.

1941 - 1945 WWII

U.S. and Britain react to occupation of southern Indochina by imposing total trade embargo on Japan. Faced with economic strangulation, Japan has the choice of withdrawing its troops or moving into the Dutch East Indies to secure oil supplies. The latter would mean war with the U.S. Prime Minister Fumimaro tries to avoid that contingency, but the militant General Tojo replaces him and initiates Dec. 7, 1941 attack on Pearl Harbor, the Philippines, Hong Kong and Malaysia. WWII enters global phase. After initial success for the Japanese forces, the tide turns in June 1942 with the defeat of Japanese fleet by U.S. Navy at Midway. A war of attrition forces Japan back to their home islands. Disruption of shipping and Allied bombing of Japan industries and cities bring about shortages of food and supplies. Bombing of Hiroshima and Nagasaki on August 6 and 9 along with the Soviet declaration of war on August 8, 1945 bring Emperor Hirohito to order army to cease fighting on August 14.

1945 - Present Postwar Japan

Under the command of U.S. General Douglas MacArthur, the Allied forces occupy Japan from 1945 to 1952 and orchestrate political, social and economic reforms. As troops and civilians return from overseas, the nation experiences shortages of food, housing, clothing, goods and services. Korean War (1950 - 53) increases Japanese exports and leads to a peace treaty and a mutual defense treaty with the U.S. Full sovereignty gained in 1952. Okinawa is returned to Japan in 1972. Japan imports modern technology and makes economic development chief priority. By early 70s, Japan is a leading producer of ships, cars, steel, and electronic equipment. Japan establishes diplomatic ties with China in 1972. In the 80s, Japan plays an increasingly visible role in global affairs, becoming the largest provider of development aid in '88 and sending troops to join the UN peacekeeping efforts in '92. The death of Emperor Hirohito in Jan. 1989 marks the end of the Showa era, ushering in the Heisei era with the succession of his son, Akihito.

Main source: Grolier's Multimedia Encyclopedia. Grolier Electronic Publishing: Danbury, CT, 1993.

Christian History in Japan

In 1549, after three years of foreign missions in India, Francis Xavier set out for Japan. Xavier, cofounder of a Jesuit missionary organization, set foot on Southern Kyushu, accompanied by three Japanese and two other Jesuit priests, to open the first era of Christianity in Japan under the Roman Catholic banner.

Although Xavier was in Japan for only two years, his stamina, zeal, audiences with both lord and commoner, willingness to suffer physical hardships, and the forthrightness of his preaching established a zealous core of followers. A long period of civil war and fighting between Buddhist sects had left the people poverty-stricken, crushed in spirit and desperate for any change which signified hope. Where Japan's religions were incapable of providing such, Catholicism brought with it fresh promise.

The Jesuits offered a religion with a freshness and fervor that quickly captivated the imaginative and impressionable people. Unfortunately, within the first three decades after its introduction, the Catholic Church had adopted extreme methods to advance the Church. They used Buddhist and Shinto religious paraphernalia and encouraged strongman tactics by feudal lords to coerce their subjects to convert to Catholicism and become *Kirishitan*.

By 1582, Hideyoshi, a brilliant but ruthless dictator had come to power. After a period of acceptance of the Jesuits, he began to suspect them of political intrigue. In 1587 he ordered the expulsion of all the Jesuit priests. The decree was not fully enforced and Hideyoshi permitted them to remain as long as they behaved with moderation. Six years later, Dominican and Franciscan missionaries arrived from Manila and began work, ignoring the edict forbidding Catholicism in Japan. Once quarrels started between the rival missionary groups, Hideyoshi became more aggravated. Things came to a sudden climax when, after the beaching and subsequent pillaging of his Spanish galleon, the captain, in a fit of anxiety, tells the local lord that the powerful King of Spain expands his kingdom aided by those in the new land who have been converted to the Catholic faith. The news of this "threat" reached Hideyoshi, and served to confirm his suspicions. His reaction was explosive.

In the ensuing years, the persecution of Christians began. On February 5, 1597 twenty-six martyrs were executed on crosses in Nagasaki. Throughout the next 30 years, there were many instances of torturing and executions. Between 1614 and 1635, as many as 280,000 are thought to have been persecuted for their belief. The majority of the nominal Christians recanted their faith and entered the Buddhist ranks. But many died the martyr's death — perhaps as many as 6,000. In 1637, a religious revolt of the peasants was crushed, resulting in the death of 37,000 Christians.

During the Tokugawa Shogunate a special police commission was organized and each year the Buddhist priests were required to report whether or not any Christians were known to live in their area. Believers were required to tramp on a picture of Christ or Mary or be punished. An unrelenting period of persecution persisted for the next two and a half centuries, lasting until 1853. It was with this bitter hatred and ruthless suppression that the first Roman Catholic era came to a close in Japan.

When Commander Perry arrived in 1853, Japan was ripe for a change. In 1858 a commercial treaty with the USA was ratified. In 1859 Japan's ports were opened to foreign ships and within four months, seven Protestant missionaries landed. They found the name of their Lord intensely despised throughout Japan. Although anti-foreign feeling prevailed for several more years, the Protestant church was not slow to make the most of its God-given opportunities. In 1864, the first convert was baptized and in 1872, the first Protestant church was organized in Yokohama. By 1873, almost all major Protestant denominations had sent missionaries to Japan after the edict against Christianity was removed. Believers were drawn mainly from the samurai and upper middle class.

The period from 1883 - 1889 was marked by revival and rapid growth of the Protestant Church. The predominant emphasis was spiritual, with much prayer and dependence on the Holy Spirit. From 1890 until the end of the century, the Church was tested by reactionary, anti-Western nationals and by the rise of rational humanism and new theologies. This served to drive the true believers deeper in faith and practice. After the third general missionary conference at the turn of the century, the way was paved for a new era of inter-mission and interdenominational cooperation. The first Federation of Christian Churches in Japan was organized in 1911. The Protestant Church, once again, went through a season of growth.

In the 1930s the second of the post-restoration anti-Christian waves occurred, fueled by the hostile propaganda of right-wing nationalists and militants. This resulted in the imprisonment of a number of pastors and leaders in the early 1940s

In 1941, responding to tightening government controls, most of the denominations severed connections with mission societies and formed the United Church of Christ in Japan. In December, 1945, soon after Japan's surrender, laws were passed that allowed religious freedom for the first time in Japan's history. The effects of Japan's defeat in the war, the allied force's occupation, and the Emperor's denouncement of his divinity laid the groundwork for another season of growth in the Christian Church. In the years since, the Christian Church (including Roman Catholics, Orthodox and Protestants) in Japan has grown at a rate of about 4% per year from 340,000 members to a current estimate of just over 1,000,000.

Main Sources: ed. A. Reynolds, *Japan in Review, Japan Harvest Anthology 1955-1970*, Vol I. Tokyo: JEMA, 1970.

H. Trevor, *Japan's Post-War Protestant Churches*. 1993.

Brent Droullard
Japan Missionary

Post-War Church in Japan

1945 *Japan's Defeat in WWII.*
Tokyo Branch of Far Eastern Broadcasting Company (FEBC) opened.
1946 *Declaration of Humanness of the Emperor.*
Presentation of Bibles and hymn books from USA.
The Christ Weekly newspaper started.
1947 KGK (Japan IVCF) started.
Evangelical Missionary Association of Japan (EMAJ) started.
The new constitution of Japan established.
1948 Japan Protestant Fellowship established.
National Council of Churches of Japan started.
1950 Japan Evangelical Fellowship founded.
Word of Life Press founded.
Start of Lacour Music evangelism.
1951 Pacific Broadcasting Association founded.
Japan Bible Christian Council founded.
Religious Juridical Person Law enacted.
Peace treaty for Japan.
1952 *May-Day incident at Nijubashi of the Imperial Palace.*
1953 World Conference of Youth for Christ held in Tokyo.
Every Home Crusade started.
1954 Colloquial Translation of the New Testament (JBS) published.
1955 Colloquial Translation of the Old Testament (JBS) published.
1956 Dr. Billy Graham's first visit to Japan.
Japan admitted to United Nations.
1957 Japan Evangelistic Crusade started (Dr. Koji Honda).
1959 Centennial of Protestant Mission in Japan.
Biblical Faith Movement (JPC) launched.
1960 Japan Protestant Conference (JPC) founded.
Japan-US Security Treaty.
1961 Tokyo Christian Crusade with Bob Pierce.
Japan Council of Evangelical Missions founded.
1962 Japan Keswick Convention started.
1964 *Tokyo Olympic Games.*
1965 New Japan Bible, *Shin Kaiyaku* (New Testament) published.
1967 First Billy Graham Crusade in Tokyo.
The Christian (Evangelical newspaper) started.

1968 EMAJ reorganized as Japan Evangelical Missionary Association (JEMA).
Japan Evangelical Association (JEA) founded.
1969 Japan Mass Mobilization evangelism founded.
1970 Evangelistic Crusade in Osaka.
Japan Evangelical Theological Society founded.
International Exposition in Osaka.
1971 Japan Overseas Missions Association founded.
*Judicial decision: Shinto purification of Tsu City government building
site unconstitutional.*
1972 *Red Army incident.*
1974 First Japan Congress on Evangelism in Kyoto.
1977 *The 1971 Tsu City ruling overturned in Supreme Court.*
1978 Japanese translation of Living Bible published.
Narita International Airport opened.
1979 Tokyo Christian Institute founded (Merger of Tokyo Christian College,
Tokyo Christian Theological School and Kyoritsu Women's Bible
School).
1980 Second Billy Graham Crusade in Japan.
1982 Second Japan Congress on Evangelism in Kyoto.
1983 New building of Ochanomizu Christian Center completed.
1985 Parachurch Association in Japan founded.
1986 Reorganization of Japan Evangelical Association.
1987 JEA accepted as member of World Evangelical Fellowship and Evangelical Fellowship of Asia.
1988 *Tunnel between Honshu and Hokkaido (Seikan Tunnel) completed.*
1989 Churches protest against use of public funds for emperor's funeral.
1991 Third Japan Congress on Evangelism in Shiobara.
1993 All-Japan Koshien Revival Mission.
1994 Third Billy Graham Crusade in Tokyo.
1995 Kobe Earthquake.
AUM sect incidents.

First published in JEA *Japan Update*, Fall, 1995

Nihonkyo

What is it that has so hindered the gospel in Japan over the years? Probably it is a converging of many factors, but one key subliminal pressure that affects every Japanese who considers Christ is *Nihonkyo*.

Nihonkyo as an Integrating Web

Ninhonkyo (Japanism), a central part of the Japanese worldview, can be seen as a major reason for Japanese resistance to the gospel.

It is pervasive, manifesting itself in scores of forms, thus making it difficult to identify. It can be seen as a web integrating worldview assumptions and their related beliefs and behaviors.

Very few Japanese seem to know or care about the purpose, meaning or doctrines of Buddhism or Shintoism, yet consider performing the rituals highly important. They speak of these as just "custom," yet uphold them faithfully. Examples include Shinto blessings for crops, land, buildings, cars, children, the new year; ancestral altars, god shelves, amulets, and religious festivals. Syncretization of Buddhism, Shintoism and ancestral veneration is considered natural.

Many people do not seem to care about the emperor, and yet it is unforgivable to speak against the emperor in any way. Japan continues to name and number each year according to the emperor, starting over with each reign. Outside of the political right wing, little sentiment is aroused by the flag or the national anthem, yet there remains strong attachment to the nation.

Christianity is considered un-Japanese. Many Christians are afraid to express their faith to family and friends. Concern about what others think, guides, binds and to varying degrees dominates daily life and decisions. The opinions of others are often taken more seriously than principles of right and wrong. There is frequent divergence between what people say and do and what they think and feel.

Many pastors and believers capitulated to the government before and during World War II. After the war, the majority of pastors and lay people did not seem to see a need to repent of this compromise.

A people who have borrowed heavily from others, Japanese still insist that they are particularly unique. Their manufactured products are of high quality. Their massive trading surplus, and much examined business practices seem to have reasons rooted deeper than the economic and political. The crime rate has been low and social behavior orderly. All of the above are linked by a pervasive theme: *Nihonkyo*.

Origins and Expressions

Nihonkyo developed during the Edo (1600-1867) and Meiji (1868-1911) periods. Commoners were disarmed, oppressed, forced to obey authorities and were molded to a collective mentality. Cohesion was maintained through shame consciousness.

The Tokugawa Shogunate codified a system known as the *goningumi* (five person group). In every village the head of each household was grouped with the heads of several other households. Each maintained surveillance over the others.

A second force came from the Shinto scholars who put forth the idea that Japanese were by nature superior to others by way of their understanding and practice of "natural principles of righteousness." The Emperor was exalted as a god, obeisance to Shinto became a civic duty, and ancestral veneration was politically enforced. The coalescence of the two foundations has given the patterns of *Nihonkyo* an almost unshakable place in the culture. This was done essentially to control the people and maintain power.

Nihonkyo-Kirisutoha "Japanese Christianity"

In Japanese thinking, religion is a "tool" for gaining one's goals and is subordinate to human relationships. In this framework, to insist on Christian absolutes is nonsensical. So Christians are often said to be "more Japanese than Christian." While this priority of ethnicity may be true of Christians in any nation, *Nihonkyo* seems to exonerate this as the proper way for a Japanese. The concept of *Nihonkyo-Kirisutoha* may help explain why the church in Japan often appears so Western on the surface and yet is so Japanese, to the point of being more Japanese than Christian, at the core.

A Summary of *Nihonkyo*

If *Nihonkyo* has a theology, it is likely the Shinto tradition of the sun goddess Amaterasu, who is the mythological creator of Japan and ancestress of the emperor. The emperor's lineage is said to be the ultimate origin of all Japanese. This is fused with ancestral veneration, both on the family and national level.

Nihonkyo is tolerant of any religious belief, as long as it does not prevent one from fulfilling one's obligations as a Japanese. Conformity is critically important, not just to a single group, but to the whole social fabric of groups. *Nihonkyo* both expects and facilitates imported beliefs, customs, or products to become Japanese. Religiously, this requires syncretization, to which biblical Christianity has always been resistant. As attractive as Christianity may be, *Nihonkyo* rejects it as fundamentally incompatible and therefore unacceptable.

However untrue, this web of core value assumptions stretches across the Land of the Rising Sun and seems to be the most comprehensive way of understanding how, in this nation, "the god of this age has blinded the minds of unbelievers" (2 Cor. 4:4). If the church in Japan is to see significant growth, it must distinguish its identity as Japanese from that which is espoused by *Nihonkyo*. The church must also carefully discern and renounce *Nihonkyo-Kirisutoha* and replace it with wholehearted commitment to New Testament Christianity.

Peter Lundell
World Outreach Missionary, 1990-1996

日 本 Japan

Capital: Tokyo
Population: 124,914,373
Cities: 664
  With 0 churches: 8
  With 1 church: 75
Towns/Villages: 2,568
  With no churches: 1,750
  With 20,000 pop. &
  no churches: 77

Size: 377,682,000 km^2
Density: 150 people/km^2
Churches: 7,726
Church per pop.: 1:16,168
Worship attendance: 268,217
Attendance/church: 35
Attendance/pop.: 0.21
Member/pop.: 0.43
Missionaries: 2,224

Geography

Japan is an island country situated off the east coast of Asia in the northwest of the Pacific Ocean. The territory of Japan includes, from north to south, the Aleutians, the Kuriles, the Japanese Isles, and the Seinan Islands. There are four main islands, and they are, in order of their size, Honshu, Hokkaido, Kyushu, and Shikoku. These four islands and 3,000 others form an arc about 3,300 kilometers long from Minami Chishima to the Yaeyama Islands. A series of mountains crowd an already narrow landscape, and numerous volcanic ranges run through it, forming intricate and sometimes problematic geographical features. Most of Japan experiences the four distinct seasons of the year.

Cultural Background

Japan's official history did not begin until the eighth century. However, it is known that Buddhism came to Japan in the sixth century, and prior to this, around the second or third century written language was introduced from China. By this time, the Yamato clan had become the most powerful clan in the nation, and the chiefs of the clan are considered the ancestors of Japan's imperial family. There has been much debate concerning the origin of the Japanese race and language. Recently a number of ancient ruins have been discovered, shedding light on many unanswered questions.

Buddhism has had a large influence on the personal and political life of the people. A major example is the parishioner system established by the Tokugawa government which linked everyone to local Buddhist temples. Ancient folk beliefs, and Taoism and Onmyodo introduced from China, also have left significant marks on the culture of Japan. The Meiji administration introduced the policy to separate Shintoism from Buddhism and gave State Shintoism the highest position. The accompanying militarism led the country to its ill fate. Syncretistic faith provides the basic spiritual support for most Japanese.

1 Pray for the salvation of Japan. May the 125 million Japanese people in 44 million households come to the Saviour! Pray that at least 10% of the throngs who will visit the temples and shrines this morning will be led to attend a church sometime during this new year.

2 Pray for Japanese living abroad (over 689,000 in 1994). Pray for the Japanese churches in different parts of the world (over 315). Pray that the Christians who have found faith abroad, or have become interested in the gospel, be able to be integrated into churches in Japan.

3 Pray for the approximately one million foreign people living in Japan. Probably more are Christian than the percentage of Japanese. However, many are only nominal Christians. Others come from countries that are closed to the gospel.

4 Pray for the Japanese Christians, for the 270,000 Protestants who regularly attend worship and for the 540,000 church members, that each may grow and be obedient to the Lord. Church membership is only 0.43% of the population.

5 The Bible teaches us to "pray for the king." Let us pray for the emperor and his imperial family who are still the main spiritual support for a majority of the Japanese people. Pray that this year they may read the Bible, and be attracted to the King.

6 Pray for "all leaders in high positions." Pray for the salvation of Cabinet members, Diet members, local councilmen, and other government employees. Pray for the Christian politicians and government workers that they might represent Jesus well.

7 Pray for the Japanese financiers and businessmen. May their wealth be used in righteous ways! Pray for the owners and presidents who head Japan's two million businesses, that many become Christians.

8 Pray for the scholars and educators. Pray that the professors and researchers wisely use their knowledge, and that they come to the Fountain of All Wisdom.

The number of registered alien residents in Japan totaled 1,362,371 at the end of 1995, accounting for a record 1.09% of the country's population. South and North Korean residents totaled 666,000; Chinese residents were 223,000; Brazilians 176,000. Foreign residents in Tokyo totaled 247,000, followed with 210,000 in Osaka Prefecture and 108,000 in Aichi Prefecture.   *From Yomiuri Newspaper, 6/23/96*

北海道 Hokkaido

Capital: Sapporo
Population: 5,684,842
Cities: 32
  With 0 churches: 2
  With 1 church: 3
Towns/Villages: 180
  With no churches: 117
  With 20,000 pop. & no churches: 4

Size: 83,519 km^2
Density: 68 people/km^2
Churches: P 391, C 70
Church per pop.: 1:14,539
Worship attendance: 10,743
Attendance/church: 27
Missionaries: 140

Geography

Hokkaido in the northeast corner of Japan is the largest of all the prefectures. It is the second largest island, almost twice the size of Kyushu. It is about the size of Switzerland and Denmark combined. The distance from north to south and east to west is about equal, 450 kilometers. The island has many volcanic plateaus, and forests thrive on the mountain slopes.

Industry & Economy

Hokkaido leads or is in the upper ranks of all the prefectures in most aspects of agriculture, forestry, fishing and mining. In recent years, due to the energy revolution and changing industrial needs, Hokkaido has been facing a slowing economy. Many mines have closed down and basic industries like steel, shipbuilding, fisheries and ranching are suffering. However, with its many natural resources and wide open spaces many of these problems can be overcome.

Cultural Background

The Ainu people, known to ancient Japan as the Ezo, are believed to have been located throughout Japan's islands during the Jomon era. They are also believed to share the same ancestry as the Japanese. The relationship between them, and how separate societies were established is uncertain. In the Kamakura era, many Japanese migrated to Hokkaido. In the Edo era, the Matsumae feudal clan came to power, monopolized the trading rights, and controlled the southern part of the island. The whole island was later taken under the direct control of the Edo Shogunate as Japan's territory. During the Meiji era Hokkaido became a prefecture, and since World War II comprehensive plans have helped to develop the area.

Religious Milieu

In many ways Hokkaido is a fertile receptor for the gospel. In contrast to the rest of Japan, the culture is not tied to a long conservative history. Its ranching and farming industries, along with its spaciousness and recent immigrant history have made it more receptive to Western influence. On the other hand, the strong influence of past nationalistic Shintoism is felt through the Hokkaido Shrine. Here the people find a unifying force and help in time of need. Revival of Shinto festivals can be seen throughout the island.

The Mission

During the Edo era, many believers fled persecution, only to be captured at the Matsumae Peninsula and put to death as martyrs. In 1861, shortly after the opening of seaports, an Orthodox Russian priest, Nicolai, landed at Hakodate. Christianity was still prohibited in Japan at the time, so he spent his time studying the country. In 1869, he established his ministry headquarters in Tokyo, but expanded his work to Hokkaido and Tohoku. Dr. William Clark's work has also had a great Christian influence in Hokkaido. His famous motto, "Boys, be ambitious for Christ!" has inspired countless numbers of youths. Thanks to many postwar foreign missionaries, a solid foundation for the gospel has been established.

9 Thank God for the faithful ministry of those who have pioneered the work here. Pray that these gospel seeds will spring up throughout the island. Pray for the churches without pastors, and for those facing hardships because of the severe winters, the population decline and economic difficulties.

10 Pray for the Christian educational institutions like Iai Gakuin (girls' jr high and high school in Hakodate); Hokusei Gakuen (college, girls' jr college, high school, girls' jr high and high school in Sapporo; high school in Yoichi; jr college in Wakkanai); Rakuno Gakuen (college, jr college, high school in Ebetsu), etc.

11 Pray for Christian medical ministries like Tenshi Hospital (Sapporo), Luke's Hospital (Sapporo), Gloria Clinic, Blue Cross Samaritan's Hospital. Pray for Christian social ministries like Shinaien (Sapporo), Hokkaido Katei Gakuen (Engaru).

12 Pray for the Hokkaido Christian Center (Sapporo), Hidaka Bible Camp, Morai Christian Camp and other facilities that they be effectively used by God. Also pray for the Life Center stores (Sapporo, Asahikawa, Hakodate), CLC and other Christian book stores.

13 Pray for the blessing of the Hokkaido Missions Consultation and the coming Hokkaido Missions Congress. Pray that the gospel may spread to the remote areas through programs by the Hokkaido Mass-Communications Evangelistic Center, the TV broadcasts of *Life Line*, and the radio ministry of *Light of the World*.

Students and Youth

Children used to be a large part of Japan's population, but the number is drastically decreasing despite the country's wealth and prosperity. In the last ten years the number of children 0-14 years old has decreased 23%, while those 15-64 years old have increased 5%. In spite of these figures, we must continue to minister to the young people, for they soon will become the leaders of Japan's society.

Japan has the world's highest percentage of school enrollment. Elementary and junior high school education is compulsory, but even the other levels are amazingly high. A high percentage of smaller children enroll in preschools and kindergartens. 95% of the junior highers go on to high school and 81% of them continue to post-high school studies. An aggressive ministry needs to be implemented for the age group from 15 to 23 years old. This age bracket seems to be more receptive to religion than any other age group. Please pray that many youth will come to Christ, and also hold up those who minister to these youth.

January 15th is Adult Day (Coming of Age Day), a day on which those who have become 20 are especially honored at the city hall, the shrines and some churches. Intercede for these college-age students and for the Christian workers who seek to minister to them.

14 Pray for the *Kirisutosha Gakusei Kai* (KGK, similar to Intervarsity). It was begun by Japanese Christian students in 1947, and is active on about 250 college campuses through Bible studies, prayer meetings, summer camps, etc.

15 COMING-OF-AGE DAY
Pray for Japan Campus Crusade for Christ (JCCC). It was reorganized in 1984 to evangelize and train college students. There are 41 missionaries and 27 Japanese staff active in Tokyo, Okinawa, Nagoya, and Osaka. The summer program brings 400 to 2,000 Korean Christians to Japan for church-based evangelism.

16 Pray for The Navigators, a discipleship-centered group. There are 26 Japanese and 21 foreign staff working in ten different cities in the Tohoku, Kanto, Shizuoka and Hanshin districts. The ministry includes working with students (ten campuses), business people and families.

17 Youth with A Mission (YWAM), an international missionary organization, is active in the Tokyo and Osaka areas with various programs, including youth ministry, discipleship training, and church-planting.

東北 Tohoku District

Population: 9,865,006	Size: 66,361 km²
Cities: 63	Density: 149 people/km²
With no churches: 1	Churches: P 528, C 86
With 1 church: 7	Church per pop.: 1:18,684
Towns/Villages: 337	Worship attendance: 13,818
With no churches: 248	Attendance/church: 26
With 20,000 pop. &	Attendance/pop.: 0.14
no churches: 8	Missionaries: 120

The Tohoku district is located in the northeastern region of Honshu Island. It is twice the size of the Kanto district. The population, however, is less than 1/3 of Kanto, slightly smaller than Tokyo itself. Except for the larger cities such as Sendai and Koriyama, local industries cannot fully support the economy, thus, people in their prime of life leave home to work elsewhere. Agricultural villages are especially losing population, a trend which probably will continue.

Fukushima is the only prefecture whose church per population ratio is better than the national average. Several postwar foreign missionary groups have done remarkable jobs in starting churches in areas where population is declining. As their believers have moved to the urban areas, the mission groups have often assisted in starting churches there also. These Christians still carry heavy burdens for their Tohoku home towns. The Tohoku area first was touched by Catholic *Kirishitan*. Then in the Meiji era the Russian Orthodox Church did an amazing job of evangelism. Tohoku has produced many capable church leaders.

18 Pray for the 528 churches in the six prefectures. Severe winters and heavy snowfall, depleting population are problems that are unique to this area. Pray that the day soon comes when young people can find employment without needing to leave. Also remember the foreign missionaries and their excellent work.

19 Pray for the 248 towns with no churches, among them the eight unchurched towns with populations of over 20,000. There are seven cities with only one church each. Obanazawa City (23,000 population) has no church. Also pray that a special strategy will be developed to reach the remote mountain villages of Iwate and others.

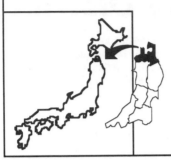

青森 Aomori

Capital: Aomori City
Population: 1,508,720
Cities: 8
  With 1 church: 0
Towns/Villages: 59
  With no churches: 46
  With 20,000 pop. &
  no churches: 1

Size: 9,247 km^2
Density: 163 people/km^2
Churches: P 75, C 15
Church per pop.: 1:20,116
Worship attendance: 1,874
Attendance/church: 25
Missionaries: 19

Geography

Aomori is located at the northernmost end of the Ou Mountain Range. It embraces the Hakkoda Mountains and both sides of Mutsu Bay, whose east side is Shimokita Peninsula and west side is Tsugaru Peninsula. The mountain range separates the area with the eastern side facing the Pacific Ocean. That area enjoys a milder winter with sunny days and light snowfalls. But at times summer brings a cold wind called *Yanasei,* and thick fog can damage the crops. The western side faces the Japan Sea and experiences heavy snow, but sunny days in the summer.

Industry & Economy

Aomori is famous for its apples, producing close to half of the nation's crop. Other important crops are rapeseed and garlic with 70 to 80% of the nation's total. 30% of the nation's canned mackerel and squid come from Aomori, the highest in the nation. However, the lack of heavy industries along with the hard weather force many to seek employment in the bigger cities during the winter. The prefecture has struggled to revitalize depressed areas. The new atomic power plant at Mutsu City was a bright spot, but the nuclear waste disposal, pollution and environmental issues have turned it into a large disappointment.

Cultural Background

Since Aomori sits at the northernmost point of Honshu the area has been called *Mutsu* (end of the road) since antiquity. Though the opening of the Seikan Tunnel joining Aomori and Hokkaido lessened the feeling of remoteness, the traditions and customs established long ago still have a powerful hold. Even in a city like Misawa with many American military bases and Japanese self-defense forces, very little has changed. A national survey showed that the people here were the most reluctant to meet new people. This shows their conservative nature and weakness in making new relationships. However, once a relationship is established, it becomes very deep and warm.

28

Religious Milieu

Religious influence is seen in many ways here. The Nebuta Festival (Aug. 3-7) is one of the three major festivals of the Tohoku area and attracts many tourists. Mount Osore is famous for the many spiritual mediums/sorceresses called *Itako*. Mt. Iwaki is also an important Shinto site for worship, and the folklore known as *Oshirasama* has deep roots in the people's faith. It is not uncommon to see whole families and communities visiting the temples and shrines during festival times, and even on ordinary days.

The Mission

A lord of the Tsugaru clan converted to Christianity during the Kirishitan era (beginning in mid-1500s), and many others followed him. At the beginning of the Meiji era Mr. Yoichi Honda became a Christian in Yokohama. He later became the first superintendent of the Japan Methodist Church. He established a special training school (To'o-Gijuku) at Hirosaki and was able to educate many Christians. Rev. Juji Nakada, the founder of the Holiness Church, is another influential Christian leader from Hirosaki. Honda invited John Ing, a missionary from America, to briefly help in the work. During that time Ing introduced apples to the area, later to become the symbol of Aomori. Postwar missionaries have done outstanding Christian work here.

20 Pray for God's blessing on each of the small groups, that they will be able to overcome the religious obstacles and severe climate, and that the Christians will have patience and power to see His harvest.

21 Pray for To'o-Gijuku (boys school at Hirosaki); Hiromae Gakuin (girls' college/jr college/high school), and other Christian schools. Pray that the first Protestant school can be established in the southern section.

22 Pray for the ministry of Ishizawa Clinic (Hirosaki), and ask that other Christian medical facilities can be established. Pray for numerous preschool programs sponsored by churches, that they will be able to effectively teach God's love and gospel.

23 Pray for the camping ministry at Aomori Christian Center, located at Moya, and for the Light of the World Bookstore and Tsugaru Literature Center, both in Hiromae City.

24 Pray that churches can be established in the 47 towns and villages without a witness. Pray for good cooperation among the churches throughout the prefecture. Pray for the Misawa Christian Cooperative Evangelistic Fellowship and the Aomori Evangelistic Broadcasting Fellowship.

Aomori is famous for its apples. Read Proverbs 7:2; ask the Lord to remember His people in Aomori with a special revelation of His grace this week.

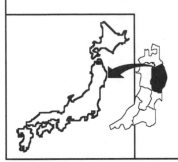

岩手 Iwate

Capital: Morioka
Population: 1,430,118
Cities: 13
With 1 church: 5
Towns/Villages: 46
With no churches: 39
With 20,000 pop. &
no churches: 3

Size: 15,277 km²
Density: 94 people/km²
Churches: P 56, C 17
Church per pop.: 1:25,538
Worship attendance: 1,278
Attendance/church: 23
Missionaries: 9

Geography

Iwate Prefecture is second in size to Hokkaido, but is the least densely populated, a prime example of a declining population area. The middle of the prefecture is occupied by the Kitakami Plateau, called Japan's Tibet, and the jagged coastline of the Pacific Ocean leaves little room for population concentration. On the west the Ou Mountain Range separates it from Akita. The Kitakami River runs through the middle north to south, creating a series of basins where the majority of the population resides. A single train line runs north and south, but the east and west transportation routes are not convenient.

Industry & Economy

Even though Iwate faces the Pacific Ocean, the fishing industry is not as successful as in Miyagi and Aomori Prefectures. The jagged coastline and the lack of good land transportation have been major hindrances.

Most of the land is too high for regular agriculture, but over 50% of Japan's gentian crop is grown on Iwate's hillsides. Iwate is also second only to Hokkaido in its lumber production. The completion of the Tohoku Shinkansen (Bullet Train) line has revitalized Morioka City. However, when the line was extended to Aomori City, the Morioka station lost the advantage of being the final destination of the line. Nevertheless, travel time north and south has been greatly reduced, helping to open up the area.

Cultural Background

Life here has never been easy due to the severe cold weather and the poor economy. The average income is 11th from the bottom, and only Aomori and Akita have worse incomes in the Tohoku area. These difficult conditions have produced many renowned figures including scholars, politicians, novelists and artists.

Religious Milieu

Ruling from the present-day Hiraizumi City in Iwate, the powerful Fujiwara clan controlled the whole Tohoku area for a hundred years, making it a "Golden era." Buddhism was the official religion, but the people mixed it with folk religion. Toward the end of the *Sengoku* era many among the Date clan appear to have converted to Christianity. When the ban on Christianity was lifted during the Meiji era, Catholic, Orthodox and Protestant missionaries began ministries here.

The Mission

At the beginning of the Tokugawa era a man by the name of Juan Goto was active in supporting the Christian work in the Tohoku area in spite of government oppression. He had some connection with the Mizusawa area in the south part of the prefecture until being banished by Masamune Date.

Rev. Tosaji Obara, who came from Towa located in the middle of the prefecture, is an example of the many fine Christian leaders from Iwate. He was part of the Holiness Church before the War, and after the War became a leader in the United Church of Christ's *Holiness no Mure*, and pastor of the Tokyo Yodobashi Church.

Although the rate of growth might not be especially high, it would be wise to concentrate on the evangelization of the more heavily populated area up and down the Kitakami River.

25 Pray that the churches located in declining population areas would be encouraged and maintain their important ministries. Pray for the faith of church members who have moved to the larger cities for education or work.

26 Pray for the evangelistic and discipling ministries of Christian schools in Iwate. Some of these schools are: Morioka University (college/jr college/high school), Mukonakano Gakuen (girls' high school in Morioka), Homare Gakuen (jr college, jr high, elementary in Kuji).

27 Christian medical facilities are rare here. Pray that more may be established. Pray for the witness at Oku Nakayama Gakuen for the handicapped, Chiisaki Mori no Sato and Sanai Gakusha High School (both in Ichinohe Town, Ninohe County).

28 Pray for the ministry of Zenrin Kan, a Christian center in Morioka, and the book store located there. It is the only Christian book store in Iwate. Pray for the radio programs, *Light of The World* and *Children of The Star.*

29 Pray that the economy may improve, allowing Christians to return to the prefecture, and providing jobs to keep younger people.

Iwate and Toyama have the lowest percentage attending worship in Honshu, 9 in 10,000 people. Read Isaiah 51:3; ask the Lord to encourage His people and make them flourish.

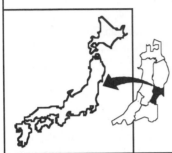

宮城 Miyagi

Capital: Sendai
Population: 2,311,572
Cities: 10
  With 1 church: 1
Towns/Villages: 61
  With no churches: 38
  With 20,000 pop. &
   no churches: 1

Size: 7,292 km²
Density: 315 people/km²
Churches: P 138, C 20
Church per pop.: 1:16,751
Worship attendance: 4,692
Attendance/church: 34
Missionaries: 49

Geography

The east side of Miyagi faces the Pacific Ocean, the west borders Yamagata Prefecture at the Ou Mountain Range; north is Iwate at the south edge of the Ichinoseki Plateau; south is Fukushima Prefecture and the north side of the Abukuma Highland. The central area has many hills and the Sendai plains. Population centers around Sendai.

The northern coastline is an extension of the ragged shoreline from Iwate. The west part of Oshika Peninsula is where Kinkazan sits extending into the Sendai Bay. Its spectacular view of Matsushima Island and Bay is known as one of the three most beautiful views in Japan. The climate is relatively mild for the Tohoku area, and the snowfall is not heavy in the plains.

Industry & Economy

Miyagi's wider plains and milder weather have resulted in its larger population. In the last few years secondary industry has been developing rapidly. Industrial parks have recently been built on the southern and eastern sides of Sendai, and harbor development projects are under way. Marine industry is ranked high nationally with the main fishing ports of Shiogama, Ishinomaki, Onagawa and Kesennuma, and oyster farming at Matsushima Bay. Agriculture is also a very productive industry. The rice harvest, including the well-known *Sasanishiki* rice, ranks 4th in the nation after Hokkaido, Niigata and Akita. Miyagi can boast of the best economy among the six Tohoku prefectures.

Cultural Background

There has been stability in the area since the Tokugawa era when it was controlled by the Date clan. In the early days of that era there was a progressive atmosphere, even to the point of sending a delegation to Rome on a cultural mission. However, under the control of the feudal government, preservation of old traditions pushed it back to a conservative mode. Sendai has now been designated as a special governmental city and is close to becoming a million people city. This rapid growth is changing the local culture, encouraging a materialistic way of life here.

Religious Milieu

After Christian freedom was restored during the Meiji era, the Russian Orthodox Church began aggressive church planting ministries, and they were followed by a number of Protestant missionaries. Many mission schools were started, especially in Sendai, and this seems to have resulted in the people there being more open to the gospel. The people of Miyagi have weaker feelings toward religion than the other sections of the Tohoku area, and consequently Buddhist and Shinto influence is not quite as strong. However, traditional religious activities such as *Tanabata* are still deeply rooted in the society.

The Mission

Much foreign missionary work has been done in the Tohoku area since the War, and a number of these groups have used Sendai as their headquarters. One of these is the Conservative Baptists. From Sendai they reached out into other parts of Miyagi, Yamagata, and Iwate, eventually establishing a seminary and a publishing ministry. Almost every Christian denomination can be found in Miyagi, with a growing number of churches able to assist more needy areas with a gospel outreach. A growing relationship of fellowship and cooperation is encouraging.

30 Pray for Tohoku Gakuin (college, boys jr high and high schools in Sendai); Miyagi Gakuin (girls' college & jr college, girls' jr & high schools in Sendai); Shokei Jo-Gakuin (jr college, jr & high schools in Natori) and other mission schools.

31 Pray for Hikarigaoka Spellman Hospital in Sendai, which serves the community as one of the few Christian medical facilities. Pray for Christian social welfare facilities for children such as Sendai Christian Kyoikuji In, Sendai Yoji In, Matsushima Kodomo no Ie. Also pray for Minami Sanriku King's Garden, a nursing home.

1 Pray for the Sendai Student Center and for the Christian Morigo Camp in Rifu. Pray for the Life Center Sendai Book Store and the Sendai Christian Book Store as they provide literature for the Christians.

2 Pray that those in Miyagi will have access to Christian TV programs. Pray for radio broadcasts, *Light of the World* and *True Salvation*.

3 Pray for the fellowship and work of the Sendai Evangelical Pastors Fellowship and for other interdenominational cooperative fellowships.

Read Matthew 16:18 and ask the Lord to build His Church in the 38 towns and villages that have no churches.

秋田 Akita

Capital: Akita City
Population: 1,222,018
Cities: 9
   With 1 church: 1
Towns/Villages: 60
   With no churches: 51
   With 20,000 pop. &
     no churches: 2

Size: 11,434 km^2
Density: 107 people/km^2
Churches: P 53, C 10
Church per pop.: 1:23,057
Worship attendance: 1,368
Attendance/church: 26
Missionaries: 2

Geography

The east of Akita faces the Ou Mountain Range. On the north is Aomori and the Shirakami Highlands. At the south is Mt. Chokai in the Kamuro Highlands, and the Sea of Japan is to the west. From east to west is about 40 kilometers, and from north to south is 160. The Dewa Highlands run through the middle, creating two different regions. The inland side includes the Odate, Takanosu and Yokote Basins. The ocean side includes Noshiro, Akita and Honjo Plains. Two major rivers, the Yoneshiro and Omono Rivers, run from east to west across the prefecture. Although Akita has warmer temperatures than the Pacific Ocean prefectures, it is hit by heavy winter snows.

Industry & Economy

Until recent years Akita enjoyed a solid economy with forestry and its famous Akita Pines and rice farming, along with healthy mining, crude oil and natural gas industries. Now there is a decline in these primary industries. Some growth is seen in secondary industries like lumber processing, lacquered furniture manufacturing (including Inagawa Town's special production of Buddhist family altars), and the production of Japanese sake with the area's high quality water and rice. There are also high expectations for development of a shoreline industrial district connecting Akita and Oga Cities.

Cultural Background

In the past when the ocean was the only way to transport large cargo quickly, the Japan Sea side was more productive than the Pacific Ocean side, but not now. The winter heavy snow is a deterrent in this area, but with the newly opened expressway and the Mini-Shinkansen train service the feeling of remoteness should be erased. The people here are as reticent and enduring as in other parts of Tohoku. Families and relatives are closely knit. According to one survey, loyalty to their prefecture is surpassed only by that in Okinawa.

Religious Milieu

The influence of the temples and shrines is deeply rooted in the lives of the people, but old traditions and customs are also important in this conservative area. In Akita, as in other parts of Japan, there was a healthy growth of *Kirishitan*. But Protestant ministry here did not start until 1884 when a missionary from the Disciples Church began a work. Generally people show little interest in the gospel, and often the interest that is shown is only on a superficial level.

In Aikita City there are two Catholic girls' schools, Seirei Gakuen and Seien Misono Gakuen, and the Seien Misono Clinic.

The Mission

As is true throughout the country, people still practice ancestor worship and have a strong sense of family structure and personal relationship obligations, things which often interfere with becoming a Christian. On the other side, when a person makes a decision, these same values work to strengthen that decision. The Catholic work of starting mission schools and ministering in the rural areas has helped to give Christianity a better image. Recently there has been a growing demand for Western-style Christian weddings even in the rural areas, and the building of a Christian facility for the elderly should help to make people more receptive to the gospel.

4 Pray that Protestant schools would be started and be used to spread the gospel.

5 Pray for Shunan Hospital, Akita Women's Home and the Green Rose Olive En in Akita City.

6 Pray that a Christian camp ground or retreat center could be established in the prefecture. Pray for the ministry of the CLC Akita Book Store.

7 Pray that evangelistic TV programs could be broadcast. Pray that the 15-minute-a-week radio program *Light of the World* may be an effective witness for Jesus.

8 Pray that God would bless the Akita City Pastors Fellowship and the Akita Prefecture Cooperative Evangelistic Association. Pray that the activities of the interdenominational ministries would not be divisive, but strengthen the unity of the churches.

Akita is known for strong family ties and relationships. Read Psalm 145:4; ask the Lord to use family relationships among believers to bring whole families to Himself.

National Founding Day

Before the War, the government selected February 11th as National Founding Day. The date was based on the myth of Emperor Jimmu becoming the first emperor of Japan. It is extremely disappointing that the selection of the day was based purely upon this ancient myth. It is also frustrating because the government continues to define Japan's history in a way to promote Emperor worship and Shintoistic nationalism. During this holiday, many Christian groups sponsor seminars and programs to discuss freedom of religion and the issues surrounding the Yasukuni Shrine where war victims are honored.

This Japanese myth and its creation story are obviously not true. In some ways the two are similar to the theory of evolution.

The Bible records true history and it is a book of truth. There have always been controversies between the Bible and evolution. Many have attempted to settle the arguments by trying to consolidate the two into one theory. Others have suggested that the two are totally different issues, and that they should never be discussed on the same level. Regardless of the debate, it is clear that the Japanese people have blindly accepted and believed atheistic evolution. They need to hear the clear truth of God's creative power taught from the Bible.

Building His Church

Our goal is for people to accept God as the Creator of all nature and Jesus Christ as Savior. In order to achieve this, each Christian needs to talk to his/her neighbors, co-workers, and friends. A desire to witness should come naturally, not out of a sense of obligation. It will come from within once we come to know and appreciate Jesus as our Savior, and understand the nature of His grace. We need adequate training for our personal faith, church life and our witness. In order to build churches, local representation of the body of Jesus Christ, each member as a part of the body needs to grow and use his/her gifts.

Evangelism and church growth need to be clearly based in the church. However, in order to do so we need good programs and materials. Cooperating with other churches in the area is also important. A fruitful and successful ministry generally should be based on many people sharing the load. Let's pray that there will be great understanding and unity between different churches and various evangelistic groups. Especially pray for the pastors and leaders of various organizations.

9   Pray for the Creation Science Research Institute. It is a body that helps Christians learn about developments in the theory of evolution. It teaches Japanese how to study the Bible, and guides them to acknowledge the Creator God and to accept Jesus Christ as their Savior.

10   Pray for the Biblical Archaeology Library Association. This group is in the planning process of building a facility that would show through displays that the Bible is indeed a book of historical events.

11 NATIONAL FOUNDING DAY
    Pray for the Evangelical Association Opposed to Government Support of the Yasukuni Shrine. This group seeks to emphasize the importance of separation of religion and state. Also, pray for the various assemblies being held to discuss freedom of religion.

12   Pray for the *Seishowo Yomu Kai* (Bible Reading Fellowship) and its groups all around the country. The fellowship promotes group Bible study discussions. Groups are made up of housewives, office workers, students, etc. God is using the groups to strengthen Christians and bring people to Christ. Also remember the many other Bible study ministries.

13   Pray for *Sodoin Dendo* (Total Mobilization Evangelism). Their goals are that everyone will hear the gospel; every Christian will be a good witness; and that every church will grow. Most of Japan has participated in the program, but pray for the several prefectures which have not yet been mobilized.

14   Pray for the *Homon Dendo Zenkoku Rengokai* (All-Japan Visitation Evangelism Association). The group cooperates to train pastors and Christians to team up in aggressive visitation and follow-up.

15   Pray for the *Kokunai Kaitaku Dendokai* (KDK or White Fields). Its purpose is to help a pastor financially for three years while he/she seeks to establish a new church.

16   Pray for the Japan Church Growth Institute. It selects 12 pastors every year and trains them for two years through mentoring and seminars. Its activities also include providing seminars and materials to help local churches grow.

February 17~21

山形 Yamagata

Capital: Yamagata City
Population: 1,254,588
Cities: 13
  With 0 churches: 1
  With 1 church: 0
Towns/Villages: 31
  With no churches: 23
  With 20,000 pop. & no churches: 1

Size: 9,327 km^2
Density: 135 people/km^2
Churches: P 71, C 6
Church per pop.: 1:17,670
Worship attendance: 1,977
Attendance/church: 28
Missionaries: 16

Geography

On the east side of Yamagata lies the Ou Mountain range with the highlands of Dewa, Asahi and Iida lying side by side in the west. The Mogami River and its valley run from south to north through the whole prefecture connecting Yonezawa, Yamagata City and Shinjo. Except for the Shonai Plain where the Mogami River empties into the Japan Sea, the prefecture is covered by mountains. This has impeded the development of adequate roads and train lines. The main mountains consist of Dewa Sanzan, Mount Zao at the Miyagi border, and Mount Azuma at the Fukushima border. These volcanoes are home to a number of hot springs. Inland winters are cold with heavy snow, and summers are hot.

Industry & Economy

Agriculture and forestry are the mainstays of the prefecture. Because of the lack of evergreens in the mountains income is limited. A high percentage of the available land is used for farming. Fruit production has been increasing as the farmers effectively use the basin land and terraces on the hillsides. Production of cherries and Western pears is the highest in the nation, and grapes, apples and watermelon rank third. Economic power is slowly shifting away from Yonezawa and Tsuruoka which flourished in the past with their weaving industry to Yamagata City and Sakata with their steel and electric industries. The economic future of Sakata looks good because of its excellent seaport, which has helped it since the Edo era.

Cultural Background

As with the rest of Tohoku, people here are conservative and enduring. They also possess deep compassion and a very strong sense of obligation, traits which make for strong faith when a person becomes a Christian. No matter how much the area becomes urbanized, there remains a deep-rooted village culture with its powerful personal relationship base. This creates a strong pressure against the Christian, pressure that is rarely experienced in the larger cities.

Religious Milieu

Japanese Buddhism and Shintoism play an important part in the people's lives. Another great religious force in the prefecture is the mountain religion, centering in Dewa Sanzan (Gassan, Yudonosan and Hagurosan). It is an ancient religion, called *Sangaku Shukyo*, and is so powerful in certain areas that even the coming of Buddhism could not penetrate it. Generally speaking traditional Buddhism is considered the family religion and controls the community daily life. Folk religion with mediums, spells and curses also is part of the community life.

The Mission

There is a noticeable trend for the younger generation to try to return to or remain in the major cities of Yamagata, such as Yamagata, Yonezawa and Shinjo. As these people seek to establish their meaning for existence, this should provide a fruitful opportunity for sharing the gospel. Also, the popularity of Christian weddings may not be just a fad, but indicate more serious concerns.

Obanazawa City (23,000 population) is one of the 8 cities in Japan with no churches. One church in the area is hoping to start a church there by 2000 A.D.

17 Pray for Yamagata Gakuin (high school) that it will maintain its Christian vision, for Christian Independent Gakuen (boarding high school) and its unique total character development program.

18 Pray that Christian medical clinics can be started. Pray for the welfare ministry to the mentally handicapped: Yamagata Hikari Gakuen and Yamagata Ikuseien (both in Kaminoyama City), Sagae Kyoro Ikuseien and Yunohama Shionen (facility for the elderly in Tsuruoka).

19 Pray for the Christian ministry of the Church of God Sakata Church Camp at Yuza, Conservative Baptist Miiko Memorial at Yonezawa, Ohira Hotel and Narisawa Pension, both at Zao Hot Springs.

20 Pray for the ministry of Life Center Yamagata Book Store and for Akita CLC and their mobile book sales in Yamagata. Pray that Yamagata will get access to evangelistic TV programs, and that the Lord would bless the three weekly Christian radio broadcasts through Yamagata Broadcast Station.

21 Pray that evangelical churches would be able to cooperate and start new churches in Obanazawa City, and in the many towns and villages with no churches. Pray for the Pastors Fellowship at Sakata City, and for the Gideon Association branches at Yamagata, Yonezawa and Shonai.

Yamagata is known for its fruit production. Read John 15:16; ask the Lord to bear this abiding fruit through His people in Yamagata.

福島 Fukushima

Capital: Fukushima City
Population: 2,137,990
Cities: 10
  With 1 church: 0
Towns/Villages: 80
  With no churches: 51
  With 20,000 pop. &
  no churches: 0

Size: 13,784 km^2
Density: 155 people/km^2
Churches: P 135, C 18
Church per pop.: 1:15,837
Worship attendance: 2,629
Attendance/church: 19
Missionaries: 25

Geography

Fukushima is the southernmost prefecture in the Tohoku area. The north borders both Miyagi and Yamagata, the south connects with three prefectures in the north Kanto area, the west with Niigata, and the east faces the Pacific Ocean. It is the second largest of the Tohoku prefectures. The plains area along the Pacific Ocean is called Hamadori. The other major flat area, called Nakadori, runs down the middle of the prefecture between the Abukuma Plateau and the Ou Mountain Range and includes the Fukushima and Koriyama Basins. Lake Inawashiro and the Aizu Basin are located in the western section. Just south of that lies the Aizu Mountain District with a line of mountains 2,000 meters tall. A variety of land conditions including the ocean, mountains, volcanoes, lakes, valleys and marshes brings a rich diversity of climates to the prefecture.

Industry & Economy

Fukushima is an agriculture prefecture, with a wide variety of produce. Apples, peaches, pears and persimmons are examples of the variety of fruits. Forests cover 70% of the area, making the prefecture the fourth largest forest region. Southern Hamadori has a few good harbors like Onahama, but because of the lack of larger harbors the marine related industry is weak. Iwaki City at one time flourished because of the Joban Coal Fields, but now the industrial center is shifting to the Fukushima and Koriyama districts.

Cultural Background

The Aizu area receives much snow in the winter due to the effect of the Sea of Japan. There is a distinct culture here, symbolized by the Byakkotai, the fighting children's army during the Meiji Restoration period. Perhaps because of this unique culture, the area has produced many important leaders in a number of fields, such as Hideyo Noguchi in medicine, Kajinosuke Ibuka and Satoshi Moriyama who became outstanding Christian leaders. The opening of the Tohoku Expressway and the Shinkansen train line are bringing new developments to the prefecture.

Religious Milieu

Even though there are few shrines and temples that are well-known throughout the nation, since the beginning of the Meiji era both Shintoism and Buddhism have become deeply rooted in the culture. Folk religion and traditional local customs and ceremonies also play a major role in the daily lives of families and communities. This religious mixture is true not just in Fukushima, but across the nation as well. In the midst of this we can see evidence of the gospel, despite strong opposition.

The Mission

Kajinosuke Ibuka was the eldest son of the Aizu clan. After being defeated in the Boshin Civil War, he moved to Tokyo where he came under the influence of Rev. Brown, one of the first missionaries during the Meiji era. God convicted him of his hate for the Satsuma and Choshu clans, and he repented and trusted Christ. He became a pastor, helped establish the Christian college, Meiji Gakuin, and later became its president. Just about that time, in 1886, the first Protestant missionary came to Aizu to begin church planting. After WWII many missionaries came to work in Aizu, Nakadori and Hamadori. Since then many ministers have come from the prefecture and serve throughout Japan.

22 Pray for Seiko Gakuen (high school in Date), New Life College High School (high school in Ishikawa) and for their important Christian outreach. Pray for Aizu Wakamatsu English Academy ministry in Fukushima.

23 Pray that Christian hospitals and clinics can be started. Pray for the Christian social ministries of Aoba Gakuen in Fukushima, Horikawa Aiseien in Tanagura, Fukushima Seishi Ryogoen in Iwaki, Sukugawa Kyoro Ikuseien, Shirakawa Kohitsuji Gakuen, Adatara Ikuseien in Otama.

24 Pray for the ministry of Christian camps and retreat centers like Sosei Group in Fukushima and Canaan Mura in Iwaki. For the Christian book stores: Life Center in Fukushima, Taira Gospel Center in Iwaki, and Kibo Book Store in Koriyama.

25 Pray that *Life Line*, an evangelistic TV program by Pacific Broadcasting shown on the Fukushima UHF channel, will continue to be shown. Also pray for the *True Salvation* radio broadcast.

26 Pray that an evangelical association of churches in the prefecture can be established. Also pray that the Evangelistic Cooperation Association will grow in vision and meaningful fellowship. Pray for the Gideon branches in Fukushima, Iwaki, Koriyama and Aizu.

Fukushima has had distinguished Christians in its history. Read 2 Timothy 2:1-2; ask the Lord to rekindle faithful discipleship and raise up exemplary models of Christian living.

Mass Media

Information media are getting more sophisticated and diversified at an extraordinary pace. The church need not be on the cutting edge of this technological whirlwind. However, it is important to use the tools that are available. Instead of one phone per household, we now have our own personal phones. Phones are useful tools for ministry, and can also be effective in evangelism. Many churches now are using "dial-a-message" types of phone outreach and follow-up.

Satellite broadcasting is now limited in total broadcasting capabilities, but cable broadcasting with its many channels will make Christian broadcasting easier. When will we be able to start our first Christian cable network? Although limited at present, within several years personal computers and internet systems will be as commonplace as radio and television.

27 Approximately 350 churches in the nation conduct a telephone ministry. A caller can hear a recorded evangelistic message by phone. Pray for these ministries and for other churches that are considering this kind of an outreach.

28 Pray for the radio ministry of the Far Eastern Broadcasting Co. (FEBC) and the TV broadcasts throughout Japan. Also remember the Japan New Media Missions Association with the support of Yodobashi Church in Tokyo. This group is actively preparing for a satellite broadcasting ministry.

1 Pray for the work of Life Line. It was begun by evangelical Christians, and has expanded to become a broader tool for helping people with various needs, even suicide prevention. Many of the volunteer staff are Christian.

2 Pray for the work of Friendship Radio, with nationwide 24-hour programing through a cable radio system. Pray that many be touched by this ministry.

Some of the Christian Programs

Radio
Bible and You (15 min. weekly)
   Features, testimony, sermon
Bible Refresh (15 min. weekly) Devotional
Bible Talk (15 minute weekly) Pre-evangelism
Children of the Star (Weekly) For children,
   especially ill children
Light of the World (5, 10, 15 minute programs)
   Japan's longest running radio program
True Salvation (10 minute weekly) Hymn/message

TV
Gospel Hour (15 minute weekly)
   Worship style
Harvest Time (30 minute weekly)
   Interview, short message
Invitation to Happiness
   (30 minute weekly) Sermon
Life Line (30 minute weekly)
   Low-key style

関東 Kanto District

Population: 39,159,557
Cities: 161
  With no churches: 0
  With 1 church: 10
Towns/Villages: 292
  With no churches: 150
  With 20,000 pop. &
    no churches: 15

Size: 32,379 km^2
Density: 1,209 people/km^2
Churches: P 2,553, C 189
Church per pop.: 1:15,339
Worship attendance: 106,549
Attendance/church: 42
Attendance/pop.: 0.27
Missionaries: 1,105

The Kanto area includes the whole Tokyo Metropolitan area. It accounts for 10% of the total national land area and 31% of the population. Centralization of population in and around Tokyo creates a number of problems. The same can be said for church concentration. The number of churches per population in the 23 wards of Tokyo is high. It will continue to grow higher because Tokyo's population has been decreasing since 1988. The population of the suburban cities and adjacent prefectures is increasing, but the number of new churches has not been able to keep up.

This population shift causes many Christians to transfer to different churches. Those who once belonged to the historic churches in Tokyo City proper are moving out and attending suburban churches. The number of towns and villages which have no churches was reduced by 14 in the last five years. There are still 150 towns and villages without churches, and 15 of them have a population of over 20,000. The total population of these 15 towns exceeds 410,000, and they have grown a total of 35,000 in the past five years. These growing areas need special attention by Kanto church planters.

3 There are now 2,553 churches in the seven prefectures of Kanto. Thank God for the 445 new churches which were started in the past ten years. This was a 21.1% overall increase and 2% annual average increase. However, in the last several years the annual average increase has settled at only 1%. The church planting growth is better in some areas, but somehow we must regain our momentum.

4 Pray for the 150 towns and villages which presently have no churches, and especial for the 15 with populations of over 20,000. Also pray for the ten cities which have only one church each. The Tochigi prefecture has the lowest ratio of Christians per population (0.24), and other prefectures with low ratios are, in order, Ibaraki, Gumma, Chiba and Saitama.

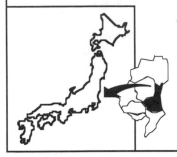

茨城 Ibaraki

Capital: Mito
Population: 2,964,839
Cities: 20
  With 1 church: 2
Towns/Villages: 65
  With no churches: 30
  With 20,000 pop. &
  no churches: 4

Size: 6,094 km²
Density: 487 people/km²
Churches: P 176, C 10
Church per pop.: 1:16,846
Worship attendance: 4,177
Attendance/church: 24
Missionaries: 46

Geography

Ibaraki occupies the northeastern part of the Kanto area. On the east is the Pacific Ocean, north is Fukushima, west is Tochigi as well as a small section of Saitama, and south is Chiba with the Tone River as the boundary. East to west is 80 kilometers, and north to south 150 kilometers. Japan's second largest lake, Kasumigaura, is in the southern part. The northern area's predominant geographic feature is the Yamizo Mountain Terrain between the Abukuma Highland and Mount Tsukuba. The rest of the prefecture is mainly flat land, the eastern area of the Kanto Plains.

Industry & Economy

Ibaraki has more cultivated lands than Niigata Prefecture, and its agricultural industry is second only to Hokkaido. The number of people engaged in agriculture is larger than any other Kanto prefecture. Because of its proximity to Tokyo which consumes so much food, the production of lotus root, Chinese cabbage, and burdock is the highest in the nation. Its shoreline lacks good seaports, limiting fishing industry potential. The prefecture is experiencing healthy growth at Mito, the Katsuta area, and the Kashima marine industrial district. It is supported by the mining industry at Hitachi with its connection to the Joban coal fields in Fukushima, and Tokai Village with Japan's first nuclear-power plant. The construction of Tsukuba Research University City has greatly improved the whole image of the prefecture.

Cultural Background

The rule of the Mito Family, one of three major Tokugawa clans, greatly influenced the cultural foundations of Ibaraki. Its ultranationalism helped during war times, but when peace came, it was a negative factor. The Mito Philosophy has promoted the spiritual life of the people, with a strong emphasis on Confucian morals, and the importance of education. This is especially felt in the northern area, centering in Mito city. The area from Tsuchiura and south serves as a commuter town for Tokyo, and with rapid population growth has a freer cultural atmosphere.

Religious Milieu

A national survey showed that Ibaraki has the least number of people claiming to have religious beliefs and it further indicated that less people believe in Buddhism than in any other prefecture. A sense of cohesiveness derived from the local community is very strong. This leads to a family religion mentality, leaving no room for individual faith. This is less true in the southern areas where there are many new housing developments. The well-known shrines are Kashima Shrine (used as headquarters by the Ancient Yamato Government for ruling the eastern area of the nation) and Kasama Inari Shrine (famous for pottery).

The Mission

As is typical for an agricultural society, people are conservative and value family relationships. This can be positive, since once the gospel takes root, people remain very faithful. The Christian work here includes the Ibaraki Christian University founded after the War. Liebenzeller Mission, and the Lutheran Evangelical Christian Church (Wisconsin Evangelical Lutheran Synod) and others have faithfully carried out work here.

5 Pray that Ibaraki Christian Gakuen (college, jr college, high school, girls' jr high school in Hitachi) remains faithful to the gospel, and grows in effective ministry. Pray for Hakujuji (White Cross) Nurses' School in Kamisu.

6 Pray for Hakujuji (White Cross) General Hospital in Kamisu; their work is one of the few Christian medical facilities in the area. Pray for Sachinomi Home for the handicapped in Tokai, Soai Home for children in Tsuchiura and the Children's Home in Naka.

7 Pray for the ministry of King's Garden at Mitsukaido; this is the first nursing home facility of an organization which is developing similar ministries in a number of locations. Pray for similar facilities for the elderly like Hakujuji (White Cross) Home in Kamisu and Aiyuen in Mito, with their long history of service.

8 Pray for Life Center Ibaraki Book Store in Mito and Itako Book Store in Ushibori. Pray that Christian TV outreaches start soon. Pray for radio programs broadcast by Ibaraki Radio: *Light of the World*, *Walking with Jesus*, and *Joyful Gospel*.

9 Pray for Ibaraki Light of the World Support Group, which promotes the broadcasting ministry, that they may effectively strengthen communication and cooperation among the churches. Pray for warm fellowship among the churches in the south, central, and north.

Ibaraki is known for its agricultural production that blesses the surrounding areas. Read Psalm 65:9-13; ask the Lord to make the Christians of Ibaraki a spiritual blessing to their neighbors.

栃木 Tochigi

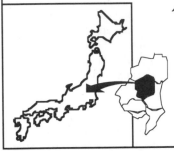

Capital: Utsunomiya
Population: 1,982,565
Cities: 12
  With 1 church: 3
Towns/Villages: 37
  With no churches: 20
  With 20,000 pop. &
  no churches: 3

Size: 6,414 km^2
Density: 309 people/km^2
Churches: P 105, C 15
Church per pop.: 1:19,187
Worship attendance: 2,473
Attendance/church: 24
Missionaries: 19

Geography

Tochigi meets Ibaraki on the east at the Yamizo Mountain Range, North is Fukushima and the Taishaku Mountain Range, West is Gumma and the Ashio Mountain Range. The middle is a wide sloping basin called Nasu Nohara. Running from north to the west is the Nasu Volcanic Chain including Nasu and Nikko. The area contains many famous hot springs and beautiful scenic spots. This inland prefecture experiences drastic seasonal and even daily temperature changes, and often suffers crop damage from frost, wind, thunder, and hail.

Industry & Economy

Agriculture is still the main industry in Tochigi, but secondary industries are gradually being developed. Specialty mining includes copper from the Ashio Mine and Oya stone from the Utsunomiya area. The main agricultural produce includes tobacco from Yamizo Mountain Terrain and dried gourd (90% of the national harvest). The textile industry that once thrived before the War is now being replaced by those tied to electronic, machinery, metal, and heavy chemical industries.

Cultural Background

Along with Gumma prefecture, Tochigi has one of the oldest traditions in the eastern part of the country. The area that depended on Tochigi was called "Shimotsuke," one of the 13 provinces of the Eastern District. The name originated around the 5th century. A survey showed that people of Tochigi scored highest in having no worries about natural disasters. They are also known to be conservative, modest, rather non-confronting, and have a relatively strict ethical code.

Religious Milieu

After the Toshogu Shrine, which had been built to worship Ieyasu Tokugawa, was transferred to Mt. Nantai near Nikko, the whole area became a sacred religious area. Even before that, the mountain had been associated with "Mountain Religion." Generally speaking, people of the Kanto area have less sense of religion. However, because of this historical background the people of Tochigi possess much stronger religious convictions, often tied to gaining material blessing. Christianity came to the prefecture in the early years of the Meiji era through young Christians from Yokohama. That foundation became the base for a number of the churches that remain today.

The Mission

Some of the churches in the prefecture are struggling. But it is encouraging to see others experiencing good growth. There is potential in the newly developed residential areas, which are relatively free from the old cultural and traditional pressures. The Nasu Plains should also provide good opportunities as the whole area develops. Well-organized plans need to be developed which will pull together various resources for evangelism.

10 Pray for Sakushinin Gakuin (college, jr and high school at Utsunomiya) and for their Christian education. The school's Shinto background has been transformed to Christian principles by the leadership of its Christian president. Pray for Asia Gakuin (Asia Rural Institute) in West Nasuno in their training of missionaries to rural areas.

11 Pray for Hiki Hospital in Utsunomiya as the staff witnesses and provides a chapel ministry. Pray for the Christian Book Center and the Book Center Logos, both in Utsunomiya.

12 Pray for the following: Koyo Vocational Center (training for handicapped at Utsunomiya). Takahara School and Ikusei School (facility for mentally handicapped at Yaita). Aishin Home for the vision impaired at Kawachi. My Home Kiyohara for the elderly at Utsunomiya. Satsuki Home at Kanuma.

13 Pray for the Christian camp and training facilities: Nasukogen House of Rest at Nasu, Nasu Seminar House at Nishi Nasuno, YMCA Shiotani Camp at Shiotani, Funyu House of Prayer (Funyu), and Yunoya Inn at Nikko.

14 Pray that people may soon have access to Christian TV programs. Pray for *Walking with Jesus*, *Joyful Gospel*, and *Path to Zion* broadcasts.

Read Philippians 1:7; ask the Lord to give the believers in Tochigi a new courage, grace and boldness in defending the faith.

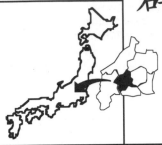

群馬 Gumma

Capital: Maebashi
Population: 2,000,623
Cities: 11
   With 1 church: 0
Towns/Villages: 59
   With no churches: 36
   With 20,000 pop. &
   no churches: 4

Size: 6,356 km^2
Density: 315 people/km^2
Churches: P 112, C 14
Church per pop.: 1:17,863
Worship attendance: 3,147
Attendance/church: 28
Missionaries: 21

Geography

Gumma is an inland prefecture in the northwestern part of the Kanto district. The northern area meets Fukushima and Niigata at the Mikuni Mountains, many of which are 2,000 meters or taller. Tochigi is east at Oku Nikko and the Ashio Mountain area; the western border is Nagano prefecture at the Joshin'etsu Highland and the Kanto Mountain district. The Tone River begins there, flowing southward to merge with the Kanna River, forming the prefectural line between Gumma and Saitama. Mt. Akagi, Haruna and Myogi are just a few of Gumma's many mountains. Typical of mountainous inland areas, temperatures are extreme both summer and winter. A northerly wind called "Joshu's Dry Wind" blows from winter through early spring.

Industry & Economy

Agriculture used to dominant Gumma, but now industrial development is growing rapidly. As a result, there are fewer people in farming than in the other two northern Kanto prefectures. The many mountains limit rice production, but it is ideal for raising silkworms, making Gumma the nation's highest producer of silk thread. Other important crops include cabbage and Chinese cabbage, both grown in the cool high mountain areas. Also, the Shimonita district is well-known for its *konnyaku* (vegetable), producing 80% of the nation's supply. Many towns stretching along the southern section of the prefecture once thrived on the textile industry, but are now becoming centers for electronic and chemical industries.

Cultural Background

There is some truth in what someone once described as the traits of the three prefectures: Gumma is "offense," Tochigi "defense," and Ibaraki "in-between." A recent excavation indicates that there was a highly advanced civilization here in the Jomon era. Pray that the wisdom they acquired to develop this high civilization be the light of their modern society. According to a survey Gumma's people are less serious about money matters, yet very practical in their outlook.

Religious Milieu

Japanese tend to carry a feeling of the uncertainty of life, but this sense is weakest among people from Gumma. Consequently, their religious sense seems to be weak also. There are no well-known temples or shrines here, but as throughout Japan, the traditional values and culture are deep-rooted. Overall, the prefecture is open to foreign culture. Foreigners make up 10% of the town of Oizumi, located in the south, making it the highest ratio of foreign population in the nation. The majority are from Brazil, many of them Catholics.

The Mission

Many Christian leaders were born in Gumma, such as Kanzo Uchimura who founded the *Mukyokai* (Non-Church) movement, and Jo Niishima who founded Doshisha University. Niishima's evangelistic efforts, centering in Annaka his birthplace, also played a key role in the industrial revolution during the early years of the Meiji era. His work was partly responsible for developing small-business owners throughout towns and cities of the northern Kanto district. Japanese and foreigners moving into the area to work in these businesses are important targets for the gospel.

15 Pray for the Christian schools: Kyoai School (girls' jr college, girls' jr and high schools in Maebashi), Niishima School (girls jr college, jr and high schools in Annaka), and Ishiguro School (business/computer/culinary in Takasaki).

16 Pray for Harunaso Hospital in Haruna and for Christian welfare facilities like the following: Megumi Garden (various facilities for the handicapped in Shibukawa) and Hanna/Sawarabi School (Haruna) for the seriously disabled.

17 Pray for orphanages: Jomo Airin-sha Chigyo Home at Maebashi, Komochi San School at Komochi. Pray for mother-child care facilities: Maebashi Home for Mothers & Children at Maebashi; for welfare facilities for the elderly: Maebashi Nursing Home, Elderly Home Eisen Garden at Haruna and others.

18 Pray for Christian training/camp facilities: Akagi Christian House, AVACO Green Village, Maebashi YMCA Akagi Camp, all at Akagi; Japan Bible Home at Minakami, Nisshinkan Manza Spa Hotel, and others.

19 Pray for Hikari Book Store at Takasaki, the only Christian book store in the prefecture. Pray that Christian radio and TV programs will be broadcast from local stations. Pray that fellowship and cooperation among evangelical churches be strengthened.

Gumma is known for its production of silk. Read Zechariah 3:4; ask the Lord to encourage the saints in Gumma with deeper knowledge of their "rich apparel" in Christ Jesus.

The Hymns of Japan

Every religion has its own music, but probably the depth of connection between music and Christianity is unique. It is hard to imagine how bleak Western music and other art forms would have been without the Bible and its accompanying faith. Jewish music originated from melody and rhythm combining with the recitation of the Bible. During the age of the Old Testament, Israel worshiped God by offering sacrifices. And the very act of praising Him was in itself called an offering. Praising the Lord is still an important part of the New Testament church worship.

The gospel entered Japan along with Western culture, and so Christianity is still seen as a Western religion. In the world of music, ancient Japanese music was looked down upon, and Western music, including hymns, easily became the music of choice. The downside is that traditional Japanese music lost its importance, and was forgotten as part of the nation's culture. In many other countries, hymnology has developed, allowing people to sing Christian music to traditional popular tunes. However, in Japan this did not happen.

The hymns sung in Japan, mostly Western, have tended to be classical high-church songs. It was not until Ugo Nakada translated many of the songs that had been used in England and America at the end of the 19th century that the church in Japan really began to sing the gospel songs. These were published as the *Revival Hymnal*. With the influence of the postwar Evangelical missionaries and the changing Japanese culture, Christian songs that were more of the folk song category became popular. Japanese themselves began to write similar songs. It is still left to be seen whether or not the Japanese church will someday be singing songs that come from the culture itself.

In Japan there are three times a year when many Japanese visit their family grave and pay respect/worship their ancestors, Obon *season in August, and then the spring and fall equinox. March 20th is the spring equinox, or* Shunbun no Hi. *This literally means "Spring Dividing Day." Our prayers should center on two targets here. First, pray for the Christians who are often in a quandary as to how to show respect for their ancestors, and yet not be worshipping their spirits. Also, pray for the many Japanese at the cemeteries. Many of them just do the ritual as a matter of custom, without any strong faith that their ancestors are listening. Pray that many will be turned to the Creator, Ruler of the living and the dead.*

20 SPRING EQUINOX (*SHUNBUN NO HI*)

Pray for the ministry *Evangelium Cantrai*. This group was established to serve churches through concerts which they conduct throughout the country. Besides their performances, the group seeks to introduce biblically based music in the churches.

21 Pray for Song Rise. This ministry is a part of Life Ministries, an American mission organization. Their work includes publishing music, seminars, etc.

22 Pray for Michtam Recording. It is set up as a business, but is committed to sharing the gospel through music. The work includes promoting concerts, music seminars, music production and sales.

23 Pray for the Tokyo Christian Choir, a volunteer choir of Christians living in the Tokyo area. They receive training and serve for special Christian concerts. Their main traditional service is performing the Messiah at Christmas.

24 Pray for Gospel World. It invites Christian singers and musicians to perform at the evangelistic music concerts, sponsors a variety of music seminars and produces CDs, tapes and videos for sale.

25 Pray for Hosanna Music, Inc., founded to support the music ministry of The Messengers, a popular gospel music group. They also sell and promote the group's CDs, etc.

26 Pray for Paravision, Inc. It produces a variety of media communication services to assist church ministries. Its business includes the production of videos, CDs, and cassette tapes. It also provides audio and recording equipment and staff for Christian gatherings.

27 Pray for Christian musicians. Some of them minister full time, but most have regular jobs and serve the Lord in music on the week ends. Pray that they may maintain high standards as musicians, but also hold to a warm Christian witness.

March 28~April 1

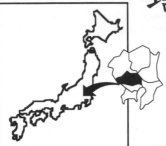

埼玉 Saitama

Capital: Urawa
Population: 6,718,268
Cities: 42
  With 1 church: 2
Towns/Villages: 50
  With no churches: 25
  With 20,000 pop. &
  no churches: 4

Size: 3,799 km^2
Density: 1,768 people/km^2
Churches: P 369, C 22
Church per pop.: 1:18,207
Worship attendance: 12,089
Attendance/church: 33
Missionaries: 218

Geography

When the old Musashi Country was divided into two, the southern part became Tokyo and the northern part Saitama. This inland prefecture is situated in the west central part of the Kanto district and covers a rather small area. However, it stretches more than 100 kilometers from the east where the Edo River borders Chiba to the west where it meets Nagano. The western region is a series of high mountain ranges including the Chichibu Basin. The east is marked by hills and highlands. The northern border has changed a number of times as the flow of Tone River changed its shape over the years.

Industry & Economy

Saitama is blessed with vast flat lands. Its percent of cultivated area is one of the highest in the nation, even though the percent of full-time farmers is relatively low. The demands of the neighboring consumer city of Tokyo boost agricultural production levels of vegetables, etc. producing significant revenue. Kawaguchi City is located in the eastern section and is famous for its metal-casting industry. Stretching north along the Takasaki and Tohoku train lines is an industrial belt which houses iron, machinery, and manufacturing industries. Besides its many modern industries, Saitama has many traditional industries. For example, nearly half of the nation's dolls used for Children's Day and Girl's Day festivals are manufactured in Konosu and Iwatsuki.

Cultural Background

The flat lands occupying much of the prefecture are being urbanized, creating the feeling that it is simply an extension of Tokyo. There are efforts to develop a pride in the prefecture itself. An example of this is the huge suburban development in Urawa and Omiya. Because of the emphasis on transportation to Tokyo, Saitama's train network joining the east and west is very inefficient. Often it is faster for people to ride into Tokyo, make a transfer there, and then go back into another section of Saitama. Another major issue is the noticeable cultural gap between the highly urbanized east and the west which is suffering from a severe population exit.

Religious Milieu

Three well-known religious sites are: Hikawa Shrine at Omiya (the principal temple of Musashi), Kitain Temple of Kawagoe (famous for its association with the Tokugawa family), and Chichibu Shrine (known for its night festivals). Mountain farming villages still maintain religious beliefs deeply rooted in folklore and superstition, and many of the younger generation and newcomers participate in regional festivities. On the other hand, many people of urban areas participate in "new religion" activities or follow heretical beliefs.

The Mission

Kyuemon Kojima started his missionary work in Sugito, located in the eastern part of Saitama. He had been in Yokohama on business when he came in contact with the gospel and was baptized by a missionary. In 1878, he started the Wato Church in his home at Sugito, and then built one of the first church buildings in Japan. Today's urbanization has had a significant effect on people's lives. Residents in the newly developed areas are relatively free from old restraints and beliefs, and often search for the spiritual dimensions that have been lost in this new life. Aggressive evangelism is needed here. The planting of new churches is scarcely keeping up with the rapid population growth.

28 Pray for Christian schools; Seibo Gakuen (jr high and high schools at Hanno), Urawa Lutheran Gakuin (jr high and high schools), Sei Gakuin (girls' jr college and college at Ageo), and Rikkyo Gakuin (high school at Niiza).

29 Pray for Omiya Central General Hospital, based on Christian faith, and Gunyokai Gospel Clinic (both in Ageo) which seeks to share the gospel through the work. Also pray for West Omiya Hospital, Futaba Hospital (Tokorozawa), Shalom Sukigara Hospital (Higashi Matsuyama).

30 Pray for King's Garden Saitama (Kawagoe) for the elderly, Aisen-en for the elderly and Aisenryo for children (Kazo), Hosanna-en for children, Kumiai-en (both in Urawa) for the mentally disabled, and other welfare facilities.

31 Pray for the television outreach programs aired on Television Saitama; *Life Line*, *Harvest Time*, and *Invitation to Happiness*. Pray that they may be effective tools for the gospel.

1 Saikyo Broadcast Missionary Association was founded for the purpose of airing *Life Line*. Pray that it may help create fellowship among the churches of the prefecture. Pray that the pastors and churches may effectively work in unity.

Saitama has 25 towns and villages with no churches as well as four cities with a population of over 20,000 people that have no church. Read Matt 9:37,38 and ask the Lord to have compassion on these people.

Seminaries and Bible Schools

Most theological schools in Japan emphasize training a person to become a pastor, missionary, theologian, or a theological school teacher. There are many different types and qualities, some outstanding and others mediocre. They have names like *Shingakuin* (theological academy), *Shingaku juku* (theological private institute), *Seisho gakuin* (Bible academy), *Seisho gakko* (Bible school), and *Seisho shingakko* (Bible seminary). Seminaries have the image of overemphasizing theological knowledge, whereas Bible schools at times are criticized for not spending enough time on theology. In order to eliminate these images, the "Bible seminary" name was created to sound like a good balance.

Some people think that theological training is not necessary, but no one denies the importance of some kind of education and training to produce Christian servants. The key to success depends on the type of education provided at these schools. Everyone knows that scholastic achievement alone does not produce good Christian servants. Often schools requiring students to live in their dormitories provide students with practical experience in praying, evangelism and character building.

In Japan, it is financially difficult to have a full-time teaching staff, so many pastors teach on a part-time basis. This provides the students with the privilege of learning practical skills required for pastoring a church as well as the educational skills.

There is a concern that the present ministerial training program is an exact carry-over from the theological courses taught in Europe and the U.S. The feeling is that a study format should be developed so as to meet the unique needs of Japanese working in a Japanese culture.

In Japan, it often makes little difference in the actual ministry whether or not a pastor has an advanced degree. There are only three universities offering master's and doctor's degrees in theology. And since these degrees only speak of the scholastic achievements of the individuals, they do not indicate the individual's faith, capability to run a church, or ability to preach.

The situation is very different in the U.S. and Britain, with advanced degrees being more needed. This kind of thinking is also influencing Japan and other less developed countries, so that in the future these advanced degrees will be more highly valued, especially for Japanese missionaries and for professors and schools which desire an international ministry. At the present time, one school that is working in this area is the Asia Theological Graduate School Japan Campus at Kobe Lutheran Seminary.

2   Pray for Tokyo Christian Institute, made up of Tokyo Christian University, Tokyo Christ Seminary and Kyoritsu Christian Gakuen. The Institute (*Gakuen*) is an evangelical institution recognized by the National Ministry of Education.

3   Pray for the training program of *Seisho Senkyokai,* previously called *Seisho Shin Gakusha* (Bible Theological Institute). The school was begun in 1958 and has two departments: church music and missions. Many ministers have gone out from the school to serve in evangelical churches. Pray that they are able to maintain their original zeal.

4   Pray for the Christianity department of Japan Christian Junior College (Chiba) and the department of theology at Osaka Christian Junior College (Osaka). Pray that both schools will maintain their evangelical position as they lead the students.

5   Pray for numerous theological schools and Bible institutes sponsored by church denominations and associations. Pray that they prepare dedicated followers of Jesus. These schools tend to be small and experience many financial and personnel struggles.

6   The Japan churches anticipate a large shortage of pastors in the near future. This is happening as the many postwar pastors pass retirement age. Pray that many young people hear the Lord's voice and dedicate themselves to the professional pastoral ministry.

7   Pray for the Bible correspondence schools that are seeking to train a growing number of older people who desire to study on a part time basis.

8   Prayer for Ochanomizu Christian Center (OCC), located in the heart of Tokyo as the headquarters of evangelical Christianity, and for its work. One of the ministries of the center is the Ochanomizu Bible Institute, which is training lay Christian leaders.

9   Pray for JTJ *Senkyo Shin Gakko* (Japan To Jesus Mission Seminary in Tokyo). The school offers a wide variety of programs which allows students to take courses on campus or by video tapes.

千葉 Chiba

Capital: Chiba City
Population: 5,778,793
Cities: 30
  With 1 church: 2
Towns/Villages: 50
  With no churches: 27
  With 20,000 pop. &
  no churches: 0

Size: 5,150 km^2
Density: 1,122 people/km^2
Churches: P 315, C 16
Church per pop.: 1:18,345
Worship attendance: 11,075
Attendance/church: 35
Missionaries: 168

Geography

The Boso Peninsula extending to the southeastern part of the Kanto Plain makes up most of Chiba. The Tone River on the north and the Edo River on the west form prefectural borders with Ibaraki, Saitama and Tokyo. The north has many old river beds and dried up lakes left by the Tone and Edo Rivers, the Shimofusa Highland in the middle, and the Boso Hills in the south. The climate is mild due to warm ocean currents, with the north very similar to the Kanto Plains. Kujukuri Beach is a stretch of beautiful sandy beach 55 kilometers long.

Industry & Economy

The percent of farm land in Chiba ranks third in the nation, next to Ibaraki and Saitama. With the Pacific Ocean on three sides and with quality seaports such as Choshi and Tateyama, Chiba has also developed a thriving fishing industry. The Keihin Industrial Belt has recently stretched along the Keihin district with landfill projects along the shoreline, making it a major hub for heavy and chemical industries. Further economic growth is projected as the Tokyo Bay crossover nears completion. The gigantic bridge and tunnel will greatly shorten the distance between Chiba and Kanagawa.

Cultural Background

Chiba has been the least culturally developed district around the Tokyo area. With the opening of the New Narita International Airport rapid growth is taking place. Makuhari Messe with its large buildings and convention facility has become a major trend-setter making the area "an exhibition arena" of modern culture. In spite of these changes the overall cultural environment is still a long way from being truly modern. Not only are people's attitudes in farming and fishing villages still very conservative compared with other prefectures in the Kanto district, but there also exists some dissension between the farming and fishing cultures. A survey indicates that people here are self-assertive and optimistic, possibly due to the mild climate of the area.

Religious Milieu

Narita Fudo Shrine, famous for its New Year's worship, attracts large crowds every year. The Katori Shrine in the north can trace its origin back to the days when Yamato controlled the Tohoku district. It was used as one of Yamato's headquarters and is believed to be as ancient as the Kashima Shrine in Ibaraki. Other famous temples include several Nichiren temples. The Tanjo Temple in Amatsu Kominato commemorates the birthplace of Nichiren Shonin, the father of the Nichiren sect. The Hokekyo Temple in Ichikawa safeguards Shonin's belongings. Buddhism is a major part of local customs, and many fishing villagers practice magic which predates Buddhism.

The Mission

The village of Hoden, now part of Funabashi City, was once used as a stopover for a merchandise freight route between the Tone River and Edo. A church was built there in the early Edo era through the work of a prominent businessman who found faith during a business trip to Yokohama and returned home with the gospel. Vigorous missionary work during the Meiji era has resulted in many large churches in the southern part of the Boso Peninsula. There is a special need to plant many churches in and around the urbanized areas.

10 Pray for Tokyo Christian Gakuen at Inzai, made up of Tokyo Christian University, Tokyo Christian Theological School, and Kyoritsu Christian Research Center. Pray for Japan Christian Jr. College (Chiba) and Chiba Eiwa High School.

11 Pray for Kujukuri Home Hospital (Yokaichiba) providing clinical services, a nursing home and rehabilitation facilities for the physically disabled and for Kaijoryo Sanitarium (Asahi) for the mentally disturbed.

12 Pray for women's shelters: Nozominomon Gakuen (Futtsu), Kanita Village (Tateyama). Pray for ministries to women and children: Asahigaoka Mothers' and Children's Home (Chiba), Konodai Mothers' and Children's Home (Ichikawa and for Yawata Home (Ichikawa) for physically disabled and Bethesda Home (Chosei).

13 Remember the ministries at the HiBA camp (Ichinomiya) and the Agape no Sato. Pray that the Lord would raise up more retreat and camp centers in the prefecture that would also effectively minister to the millions in Tokyo.

14 Pray for the evangelistic outreach of the TV broadcasts, *Harvest Time, Invitation to Happiness*, and *Gospel Hour*. Pray for the Christian book stores, Keisen Shobo (Chiba) and Aishin Shobo (Ichikawa).

Chiba is experiencing much urban, industrial and economic growth. Read Jesus' words in Matt. 6:24 and ask the Lord to help the Christians in Chiba keep their affections Christ-centered.

東京 Tokyo

Capital: Shinjuku Ward
Population: 11,542,468
Cities: 27 & 23 wards
  With 1 church: 0
Towns/Villages: 13
  With no churches: 6
  With 20,000 pop. &
  no churches: 0

Size: 2,164 km²
Density: 5,337 people/km²
Churches: P 981, C 66
Church per pop.: 1:11,766
Worship attendance: 51,628
Attendance/church: 53
Missionaries: 503

Geography

Tokyo, the capital of Japan, is one of the largest cities in the world. It is governed by two administrations: the eastern half is divided into 23 wards, and the western half is called the Tama district. The area is about 90 kilometers from east to west, and quite narrow from north to south. Most of Tokyo sits on the Musashino Plateau. The eastern section of the city lies on the northern end of the Tokyo Bay. The area is divided into the higher hills of the west, and the heavily populated eastern section. Tama River cuts across the western section of Tokyo, with the beginning of the river located all the way to the western border of Yamanashi Prefecture.

Industry & Economy

Recently many controversial issues have arisen in regard to transferring the government functions away from Tokyo city proper. The national government has been exploring various possibilities in an attempt to simplify the governmental systems, but it is too early to tell whether or not it will be possible. Nevertheless, it is very likely that Tokyo will remain a center of industry and economy. Tokyo's soaring land prices and worsening environmental problems have caused many to move away from the city proper to outlying areas such as the Tama district.

Cultural Background

During the Tokugawa era, Edo (later renamed Tokyo) grew into a city of a million people, the first ever in the world. Perhaps this phenomenon prevented true modernization of the city leaving just an artificial and materialistic culture. The people's way of thinking has not really changed much since the days of Edo. The good qualities have been lost, leaving mostly the negative. Changes have taken place in the environment, and there is quite a difference in the western mountain area compared to the urban east. The conservative practices and beliefs commonly held throughout Kanto still exist among farming and mountain villagers in the Tama district.

Religious Milieu

There are many famous temples and shrines in the metropolitan and suburban area, many which are still considered places of worship among residents: the historic Okunitama Shrine in Fuchu, Jindai Temple in Chofu, and the Mitake Shrine and Mt. Takao Yakuoin whose origins are believed to be traced to "Mountain Religion." The majority of Buddhist, Shintoist and the "New Religion" groups are headquartered in Tokyo. Christian cult groups also base their activities here.

The Mission

Paul began his missionary journey at Antioch, the great Mediterranean city of his time. He traveled extensively through the major cities, Iconium, Ephesus, Philippi, Athens and Corinth, eventually working his way to Rome. Missionary work in big cities is vital to successfully spread the gospel of Christ. As Antioch and Rome were important to Paul, so is Tokyo an important key for evangelizing Japan. There is much work remaining for the ministry.

15 Pray for the many Christian schools. Pray that they focus on the gospel truth, and not stray from the faith. Pray that they maintain healthy management and curricula. Pray that there will be adequate enrollment, and that the schools would be able to hire Christian teachers and staff.

16 Pray for the many Christian hospitals like Seishikai Hospital at Itabashi, Salvation Army Booth Memorial Hospital at Suginami, St. Luke International Hospital at Chuo, San'ikukai Hospital at Sumida, Salvation Army Kiyose Hospital with its hospice ward.

17 Pray for the many Christian social welfare programs. Pray for the day laborers who sleep at rooming houses in the Sanya district and other ghetto areas. Pray that the homeless living in makeshift shelters will respond to the gospel, and be able to return to normal life.

18 Pray for CLC Ochanomizu Book Store, Oasis Book Center in Shinjuku, Kyobunkan in Ginza, AVACO Book Center at Waseda, Tachikawa Ministry Center and other Christian book stores.

19 Pray for the Christian Diet members, and for groups dedicated specifically to pray for the government and for politicians. Pray for the Northern Tokyo Pastors Fellowship, and other groups throughout the area. Pray for the small churches that struggle especially because of the high cost of meeting places, and the busyness of the big city.

Tokyo is one of the great cities of the earth. Great grace and mercy are its immediate need. Read Jonah 3:1-10; ask the Lord to send more "reluctant preachers" to this city and ask Him to give His great mercy to the lost.

April 20~24

神奈川 **Kanagawa**

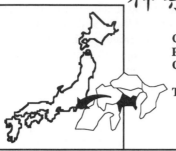

Capital: Yokohama
Population: 8,172,001
Cities: 19
  With 1 church: 1
Towns/Villages: 18
  With no churches: 6
  With 20,000 pop. &
  no churches: 0

Size: 2,402 km^2
Density: 3,390 people/km^2
Churches: P 495, C 46
Church per pop.: 1:16,509
Worship attendance: 21,960
Attendance/church: 44
Missionaries: 145

Geography

Kanagawa is the southernmost prefecture of the Kanto district. The eastern area meets Tokyo Bay, the southern area hits Sagami Bay; the Miura Peninsula lies between the two. On the north are Tokyo, Tama River and the Tama Hills; to the west is Yamanashi and Shizuoka prefectures with Hakone Volcano and the Tanzawa Mountain Terrain, standing at the southernmost point of the Kanto Mountains. Other than the mountainous areas found in the west, most of the land consists of tableland and hills. This hill country includes Yokohama and Kawasaki. As major construction continues in this area, the natural environment is disappearing. While the climate of the areas from the Sagami Bay to the Miura Peninsula is mild, the mountain areas suffer from cold temperatures and heavy rain.

Industry & Economy

Yokohama is the port city which opened its door to the outer world at the end of the Tokugawa era, and is the second largest city in the nation. The percent of people engaged in primary industry is the nation's third lowest behind Tokyo and Osaka. Agricultural and forestry industries, of course, are declining, but intensive farming methods such as nurseries and greenhouses are being effectively used. The backbone of economy consists of a variety of industries. Many are centered around the Keihin industrial district, which is gradually expanding toward the west and south.

Cultural Background

Kanagawa is the birthplace of Japan's cultural reform. Because of its international sea port and foreign influence, many progressive influences can be seen. On the other hand, there exists a strong local mentality due to the desire to be different from Tokyo. The people of the inner regions are still conservative and hold on to old traditions even though they have become part of Yokohama proper.

60

Religious Milieu

"Mountain Religion's" Oyama Afuri Shrine is famous as an ancient sacred place. Kamakura has its own share of religious history with Tsurugaoka Hachiman Shrine dating back to the 12th century. Many Buddhist temples were also built in Kamakura as a part of revival movements during the medieval period. The outdoor statue of Buddha (1252) is gigantic and impressive, and Hase Kannon dates back 500 years beyond that. The Kawasaki Taishi Shrine and Narita Fudo Shrine are two major shrines that people visit on New Year's Day. When missionaries first came to Yokohama, the people there were quite open to the gospel, already having been exposed to things international. Now churches and schools are located in the area.

The Mission

It would be advisable to more aggressively target the Yokohama and Shonan areas, taking full advantage of the relatively positive image Christianity has there. Events like "Harbor View of Christmas" show the fine cooperation of the churches in the prefecture. The newly established communities in the western part of Yokohama and the Sagamihara area should be good areas for ministry since they are free from old cultural and traditional events.

20 Pray for the many well-known Christian schools: Ferris Women's School (college, jr and high schools), Kanto Gakuin (college, girls' jr college, jr and high schools), Meiji Gakuin University Yokohama Campus, Aoyama Gakuin University Atsugi Campus, Toyo Eiwa Women's University, and others.

21 Pray for Christian general hospitals: Kinugasa Hospital in Yokosuka and Neo Gospel Clinic in Yokohama.

22 Pray for Christian social welfare facilities: Yokohama Clinic for the Blind, Japan Minakami School in Yokohama, Elizabeth Sanders Home in Oiso, Shiroyama School in Yugawara, etc.

23 Even though there are many resorts in Kanagawa, there are few Christian camping and retreat facilities. Pray for Motoyu Tamagawa Inn in Atsugi, Tanzawa Home in Kiyokawa, and others. Pray that facilities forced to close because of the poor economy may reopen.

24 Pray for the ministries of CLC, Life Center, and Yokohama Christian Book Stores, all in Yokohama. Pray for the three TV ministry programs aired on Kanagawa TV. Pray for "Harbor View of Christmas," a special evangelistic outreach.

Kanagawa is the birthplace of Japan's cultural reform. Read Acts 4:31 and ask the Lord to use the Christians to be the people of a new religious reformation that will touch the entire nation.

Scientific and Social Issues

Advances in all areas of science have raced ahead of our imaginations. One result is that scientific research is entering into areas of life which previously belonged solely to God's control. Scientists not only are declaring in a bold manner the possibility of creating life, but are also conducting highly sophisticated experiments in which they toy with life. There is a growing need for religious leaders to speak out concerning genetic engineering and human life ethics. Unless these issues are addressed scientifically, philosophically, and religiously, adequate answers will not be found.

Christianity which strays from the Bible and its authority, ends in mere humanism. As we approach the end of the 20th century, we face an increasing number of problems that humanism alone cannot solve. In these days the Christianity, which has denied the power of the Bible, has lost its voice in the U.S. and Europe. With this loss of influence in society, the role of the evangelical churches has changed drastically. The evangelicals have now accepted their social responsibilities, and with added financial and man power, have started tackling modern, social problems. Relief efforts through worldwide networking, social welfare services made available to people of all walks of life, preservation of freedom of religion, protection of human rights, defence of social justice, etc. are some of these new efforts.

Family Issues

The breakdown of the family structure is one of the biggest problems modern society faces, and is indeed the root of many other social problems. Sunday school teachers these days are hesitant to speak about family virtues naming both parents as an example, simply because the number of single-parent families is increasing. More children are growing up without fathers. Many fathers live where their job assignments are, which is often at a different location from the family. Or they spend enormous amounts of time commuting to and from work leaving little time to spend with their children.

Western culture is based on individualism, yet the Bible teaches us to respect the importance of families. One of the problems in Japan is that when we began to import Western culture, we chose to concentrate on the material aspects of the culture, without receiving Christianity and its teachings. We need to look seriously at the biblical teaching concerning the family and Christian values. These need to be emphasized!

According to 1994 Japan statistics, one couple marries every 40 seconds and one couple is divorced every 2 minutes 42 seconds. Average marriage age is rising in the case of both males (29.8) and females (27.2). Among all segments of the population, the suicide rate is highest among those aged 65 or older (31.3 per 100,000 persons). (Japan Almanac 1997, Asahi Shinbunsha)

25 Pray for PLJ, Pro-Life Japan. The organization is based on its strong belief that abortion is murder, and seeks to provide various services including abortion prevention, medical attention for the mother's health, support at child birth, and adoption placement.

26 Pray for the Japan Evangelical Association (JEA) Relief and Development Commission. The commission makes special appeals to the JEA churches to help in domestic and international relief efforts. It continues to work with the victims of the Hanshin earthquake.

27 Pray for World Vision Japan. Their efforts include a child sponsorship program, soliciting child support for poor and needy third world country children.

28 Pray for the Food for The Hungry organization. Because poverty and hunger are leading obstacles to the success of evangelistic efforts in developing countries, it sends Christians to these countries to assist in relief and development programs. It also sponsors English conversation classes in Japan, including teaching materials that inform students about poverty.

29 GREEN DAY
Pray for Diaconia Center in Sakura, Chiba, which provides various Christian volunteer activities and counseling services to those suffering from alcoholism and abortion trauma. It also works with students who have dropped out of school.

30 Pray for the Mothers' Counseling Center. This center was founded as a support system for mothers from dysfunctional families. It teaches them to raise their children with kindness and mercy in a God-loving family environment.

1 Pray for Mission 2001. The group is active in assisting churches in evangelistic meetings. It publishes Christian reading material, such as *Popo*, a monthly family-centered evangelistic newsletter, and *Upper Room*, the Japanese edition of the well-known devotional booklet. Also pray for the Youth Missions Rally held around this time every year, sponsored by Mission 2001.

2 Pray for HiBA (High School Evangelism Fellowship). Its motto is "a ministry to high school students by high schoolers." The group emphasizes leading students to Christ and then discipling them.

A total of 98,175 students dropped out of high school in 1995, up about 1,800 from the previous year. Of those, 64,431 were public high school students, representing a dropout rate of 2 percent. In private schools, the rate was 2.4 percent, with 33,478 dropouts.
Yomiuri Shimbun, 2/22/97

The Children of Japan

As modern society faces an aging problem, people have become less concerned about children. One child per household is a commonly accepted practice, and it is unlikely that this practice will change. Moreover, there are increasing numbers of couples without children. The number of households with children (under age 18, unmarried) had decreased to less than half of all households in 1980. However these trends should in no way minimize the importance of children's evangelism. Obviously, the future of our nation lies in our children. An unofficial report indicates that many Christians were led to Christ when they were children, a fact that should increase our zeal for Church Sunday school programs and Christian-based schools.

Many different kinds of children's ministries and youth work are needed. Children are more open minded to the truth. Also, today's children are experiencing many pressures from the education system and peer pressure which is beginning to include drugs and a loose life-style. They need to learn to say "no" to evil invitations, and stand for purity. Because of the many changes in the children's life style, we need to wisely update the way we do children's ministries.

3 CONSTITUTION DAY
Pray for the CS *Seicho* (Growth) Center. Its efforts include the publishing of *Seicho* (Growth), a comprehensive Sunday School curriculum. It was formerly known as Japan Sunday School Union.

4 Pray for the Japan Child Evangelism Association and its training institute. It holds *Hikari no Ko Kai* (Children of the Light) evangelistic rallies, and holds CS teachers' training seminars to help local churches in their ministries. Its mission is for children of all ages to hear the gospel and accept Christ.

5 CHILDREN'S DAY
Pray for the *Children of the Star* work. Its goal is to lead children to Jesus Christ. This group carries on nationwide ministries through a radio program, and literature, rallies and a telephone ministry. There is a strong emphasis on helping children who are suffering from illness.

6 Pray for *Chugaku Seisho Kurabu Kyoryokukai* (Bible Club Association for Junior High Students), sponsored by the Scripture Union. It teaches the truth of the Bible to junior high school students, leads them to faith, and publishes material to encourage them to read the Bible daily.

中部 Chubu District

Population: 21,286,176
Cities: 134
With no churches: 3
With 1 church: 22
Towns/Villages: 534
With no churches: 378
With 20,000 pop. &
no churches: 26

Size: 65,199 km²
Density: 326 people/km²
Churches: P 1,072, C 141
Church per pop.: 1:19,857
Worship attendance: 30,871
Attendance/church: 29
Attendance/pop.: 0.15
Missionaries: 256

The Chubu (Central) district is in the center of Honshu Island and is its widest district. It does not represent any particular political, economic or industrial boundary. It is sometimes called the Kanto Koshin'etsu Block, or the Tokai district if Mie prefecture is included. It is extremely hard to describe this district briefly due to its vast area and different land features. Plains and mountains; metropolitan areas around Nagoya and the mountain farming villages of the Chukyo area; the Pacific Ocean and the Sea of Japan. There is a striking contrast between the Tokaido Belt area and the three Hokuriku prefectures which face the Sea of Japan. These three prefectures have less than 150 churches, with only 6,351 Christians. On the other hand, the Shizuoka and Aichi prefectures on the Pacific side have 534 churches, with 31,495 Christians. These statistics are deceiving, because Aichi has more churches per population than Ishikawa but less than Toyama. Shizuoka has a slightly higher number of churches per population than the national average. Aichi has been experiencing a rapid population growth in all its cities but one, creating a great need for new churches. Twelve of Aichi's towns with a population of 20,000 or more do not have churches, the most for any prefecture.

7 Pray that the 1,072 churches in the Chubu district grow and reach out into new areas in ways that will meet the unique needs of each community. Pray that twenty new churches be started in this the most under-churched district in Japan. Pray for Ishikawa and Gifu prefectures which have had a very low number of new churches started during the last ten years. Also pray for Niigata and Aichi where there is little headway in church planting.

8 Pray that churches be started in the 378 unchurched villages and towns. In the past ten years, there have been only 1-3 new churches started in the towns and villages in each Chubu prefecture. There is an urgent need for churches in 26 villages and towns with populations over 20,000. The Pacific Ocean side with its warm climate and convenient transportation systems make it an ideal location for more Christian retreat/camp facilities.

新潟 Niigata

Capital: Niigata City
Population: 2,488,917
Cities: 20
  With 1 church: 6
Towns/Villages: 92
  With no churches: 74
  **With 20,000 pop. &
  no churches:** 3

Size: 12,112 km^2
Density: 205 people/km^2
Churches: P 97, C 27
Church per pop.: 1:25,659
Worship attendance: 2,549
Attendance/church: 26
Missionaries: 18

Geography

Niigata is the fifth largest prefecture in the nation. It is approximately 250 kilometers from the northern to the southern border. It stretches along the Japan Sea with its back border the Echigo Mountain Range. From east to west at its widest place it measures 150 kilometers. On the north tip is the Asahi Highland and the southwest tip is Hida Mountain Range, both extending into the ocean. Niigata borders five other prefectures: Yamagata, Fukushima, Gumma, Nagano and Toyama. Thirty kilometers into the Japan Sea sits Sado Island, the 8th largest island in Japan.

Industry & Economy

Niigata is second only to Hokkaido in the amount of rice it produces. Along the ocean in the sandy dune area watermelons are grown as well as tulips, a regional specialty. The Echigo Plains contain a rich reservoir of natural gas. The prefecture also is blessed with an abundance of water, generating the third highest amount of hydroelectricity in the nation. These natural resources support the shoreline industries located in Niigata City and Naoetsu. Traditional industries include western-style Tsubame tableware and Sanjo cutlery.

Cultural Background

Heavy snowfall limits the possibility of outdoor work, so many people seek work in big cities like Tokyo during winter. They are known to be hard-working. Many public bathhouses and tofu stores in Tokyo are owned by people from Niigata. Perhaps this is because Niigata people, with their strong sense of commitment to work, are willing to take on the not-so-easy jobs. Nationally, people from Niigata people are ranked highest by people around them for being reliable and trustworthy.

Religious Milieu

Extremely severe winters forced people to be resigned to their conditions, but several new Buddhist religions which came to Japan over 700 years ago provided the needed spiritual support. One of them was taught by Nichiren who was once exiled to Sado Island. The other was introduced by Shinran and called *Jodo Shinshu*. It taught that man cannot be saved by his works or prayers, but only by the mercy of *Amida*. More traditional beliefs can be seen at Yahikosan Shrine, where many gather for New Year's worship. An awareness survey indicates that people do not especially hold strong religious beliefs. It also suggests that they feel secure in their community life.

The Mission

Completion of the Joetsu Bullet Train Line and Kanetsu Express Way has shortened the travel time to Tokyo metropolitan areas. Niigata is also providing an open door to Russia and North Korea through ocean freighting and trading. This places new opportunities for evangelism in Niigata. The door is wide open. We also need to make a special effort to reach the mountain communities with their decreasing population.

9 Pray for Keiwa Gakuen School (high school and college at Shibata). The school was started thirty years ago with Christian foundations and the college began in 1991. Pray that more Christian schools be established.

10 Pray that Christian hospitals and clinics be started. Pray that if there are Christian medical facilities in the prefecture, they may become openly Christian. Also pray that Christian welfare facilities be established.

11 Pray for Christian book stores: Life Center Niigata and Seiko Book Store. Pray that evangelistic programs be televised. Pray for *Light of The World* aired on Niigata Radio.

12 Pray for Kashiwazaki Bible School. It has endured hardship for years, yet has nurtured and raised up many Christian workers. Pray that their need for staff and resources be met.

13 Pray that The *Light of The World* Support Association continues to draw churches together in healthy fellowship. Pray that Joetsu Evangelistic Association be successfully organized and become a strong basis for cooperative Christian work.

Niigata is known for a people with a strong sense of commitment and a readiness to take on difficult tasks. Read Acts 1:8 and ask the Lord to send out laborers from the churches in Niigata with a Spirit-directed commitment to the Great Commission.

富山 Toyama

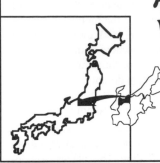

Capital: Toyama City
Population: 1,126,841
Cities: 9
  With 0 churches: 2
  With 1 church: 2
Towns/Villages: 26
  With no churches: 19
  With 20,000 pop. & no churches: 3

Size: 4,252 km^2
Density: 265 people/km^2
Churches: P 46, C 5
Church per pop.: 1:24,497
Worship attendance: 1,044
Attendance/church: 23
Missionaries: 20

Geography

The eastern section of Toyama meets Niigata and Nagano prefectures at the Hida Mountains, called the Japanese Alps. Relatively low hills border Ishikawa on the west. The southern part meets Gifu at the northern and highest tip of the Hida Highland. On the north is Toyama Bay. The Jinzu and Sho Rivers form the Toyama Plain which occupies the middle of the prefecture. The rough terrain of the Tateyama Mountains in the east has made outside access next to impossible. Heavy snowfalls in the mountains provide vital water reservoirs. The water seldom causes floods in the flat lands below. In fact, unusual dryness and gusty winds can create dangerous fire conditions.

Industry & Economy

Most of the cultivated land in the prefecture is wet rice fields, and it is well known for its shipments of early rice crops. The wide mountainous areas are not suitable for forestry industry. However, the fishing industry is booming. The harvesting of *hotaru* squid in Toyama Bay, deep sea and inshore fishing are all profitable. Seafood processing is also a very stable industry. The backbone of the economy, however, has been shifting to heavy and chemical industries. This shift can be attributed to Toyama's ample supply of water and electricity, the economic strength of factory sites, and a solid supply of laborers. Traditional enterprises of the prefecture include pharmaceuticals, apparel, and the manufacture of furniture.

Cultural Background

Toyama was once the center of Koshi Country. It was then divided into three countries: The first called Echizen (Ishikawa and Fukui prefectures), the second, Echigo (Niigata prefecture), and the third, Etchu, which later became Toyama. People of the prefecture have gone through different governing powers since the Nara era, and have learned to bond together despite the unstable political climate. They still lead a life of unselfishness, diligence, and self-denial, and are known as down-to-earth people who do not revolt against power.

Religious Milieu

As in all of the Hokuriku area, Buddhism and Shintoism are deeply rooted here. The ratio of Buddhist followers to the population is the highest in the nation. Referred to as "Kingdom of *Jodo Shinshu* Buddhism," huge numbers of people believe and follow Shinran's teachings. In contrast to other places, they do not practice Buddhism for material gain, but for deeper spiritual reasons, seeking to escape the corruption of this world. Buddhism's influence can be seen in every facet of their lives.

The Mission

Looking back on history, Buddhism is as forceful now in people's lives as it was in the past. They have endured resistance and persecution by followers of old Buddhism. History states that Buddhist missionaries enthusiastically propagated their faith even in the mountainous areas in back of Gokayama and successfully converted the people. Christian missionary work now faces the same hurdle that those missionaries had to overcome. In recent times a foreign missionary learned that Toyama was one of the least evangelized areas in Japan, and was led to establish the first church in Himi City. It is hard to break down the defenses, but when they do receive the faith, they often are solid committed believers.

14 Presently there are no Christian schools in Toyama. The prefecture has a very difficult religious climate, so the need is very great. Pray for the testimony of Christian students enrolled in colleges and vocational high schools. Also, pray for the four church-affiliated kindergartens in the prefecture.

15 Around the world in countries where Christianity is forbidden, medical missions have been effective. Pray for a Christian medical service to be started and become an effective tool here. A Christian hospice ministry is also needed.

16 Pray for three church-affiliated day care centers. Christian social ministries are hardly available in the prefecture. Pray for the witness of Christians who are working in secular welfare programs.

17 There are no Christian book stores or training/camping facilities in the whole prefecture. Pray that effective ministries be started. Pray for *The Light of The World* and *Bible Talks* aired on North Japan Radio.

18 There are 19 towns and villages located in the mountain areas of Tateyama and Gokayama which have no churches. The two unchurched cities are Namerikawa City (32,000) and Shin Minato City (39,000).

Toyama is known for its booming fishing industry. Read Matt. 4:19 and ask the Lord to make the Christians of this prefecture fishers of men.

石川 Ishikawa

Capital: Kanazawa
Population: 1,171,986
Cities: 8
  With 1 church: 2
Towns/Villages: 33
  With no churches: 24
  With 20,000 pop. &
  no churches: 1

Size: 4,197 km^2
Density: 279 people/km^2
Churches: P 55, C 8
Church per pop.: 1:21,309
Worship attendance: 1,724
Attendance/church: 31
Missionaries: 6

Geography

Ishikawa is in the middle of Honshu Island facing the Sea of Japan. The Noto Peninsula occupies the north half, and the south half meets Toyama and Gifu prefectures at the Hodatsu Hills and the Ryohaku Mountain region. The Hakusan mountains extend toward the ocean and become a hilly area, where they meet Fukui prefecture. Weather is typical for the west coast. There is much rain in winter and summer, and excluding the shoreline, the area experiences heavy snowfall. Natural disasters including typhoons are infrequent, making it a pleasant place to live. Hakusan Volcano Chain runs through the prefecture and provides many hot springs along its ranges.

Industry & Economy

The Kaga Plain in the center of the southern part is the home of Kaga rice. It is an early rice crop which is shipped to other areas of the country. Noto Peninsula produces dry field crops and fruits, but it is hilly with its cultivated acreage very limited. The agricultural produce ranks below Toyama and barely above Fukui. But its fishing industry is successful because of good seaports on the Noto Peninsula. Seafood production is ranked 19th in the nation, and 3rd among the west coast prefectures. The traditional industries include lacquer ware, ranked first in the nation, and ceramics such as Kutaniyaki.

Cultural Background

Ever since the Sengoku era, when Ishikawa prefecture was under control of the Maeda family, people's lives in this prefecture have been very stable. *"Kaga Hyakuman-goku* (million rice bags)" literally tells the healthy economic condition of the prefecture. People are conservative and somewhat negative, partly due to the climate; wintry cold, heavy snow, and a lack of sunshine. They demonstrate great patience. An awareness survey indicates that these people are more satisfied with their present way of life than any other place in Japan.

Religious Milieu

Jodo Shinshu Buddhism was the main spiritual energy for people during the Kamakura era, before the Maeda rule began. Riots led by *Jodo Shinshu* believers spread throughout Hokuriku. Even after they lost control over their lands, *Jodo Shinshu* ruled their faith. Ishikawa is called "Kingdom of Buddhism", and it is very common to see people attending weekly Buddhist sermons and Sunday schools. As is typical of Buddhist development, their belief is blended with ancient Shintoist and primitive folklore beliefs, with the various regional religious festivities reflecting this syncretism.

There are hardly any Christian educational or medical facilities in the whole area. Kanazawa Holy Spirit General Hospital (Catholic) is the only Christian medical facility in Ishikawa.

The Mission

In the 16th century when Christianity began to be suppressed, Ukon Takayama was placed under house arrest at the residence of the Maedas. Against all odds, he continued on with his mission, starting a church and a theological school. Over 1,000 people were converted during 25 years of ministry until his exile to Manila. In the early years of the Meiji era, many missionary efforts were undertaken. During the mid-Meiji period, Methodist churches were actively engaging in mission work throughout the Hokuriku district. Their activities continued after the War and are still extremely strong, giving encouraging signs of hope.

19 Hokuriku Gakuin (jr high/high school, women's jr college at Kanazawa), formerly known as Kanazawa Women's School, was founded in 1885; it remains as the only Christian school in Hokuriku. Pray that they be faithful and continue to prosper. Also remember the several church-affiliated kindergartens.

20 Pray for children's welfare facilities such as Baiko Children's Home at Kanazawa, Shio Children's Home at Shio.

21 Pray for CLC Books Kanazawa Store. Another book store, Fukuin Kan, started in a Methodist church, continues in Kanazawa, with publishing done in Tokyo.

22 Pray that the Hokuriku district may have evangelistic TV soon. Pray for *The Light of The World* aired on Hokuriku Radio. Pray that the program becomes an effective tool for the gospel.

23 Pray for the Noto Bible Church whose facilities are used for a retreat center, accommodating sixty. Pray that evangelical churches have good cooperation through the fellowship of *The Light of The World* Support Group and the Hokuriku Missions Congress and other fellowships.

Ishikawa is called the "Kingdom of Buddhism." Read II Corinthians 10:4, 5 and ask the Lord to give Christians a new faith and knowledge of their position in Christ as they confront the powers of darkness.

福井 Fukui

Capital: Fukui City
Population: 826,407
Cities: 7
  With 1 church: 1
Towns/Villages: 28
  With no churches: 19
  With 20,000 pop. &
  no churches: 0

Size: 4,192 km²
Density: 197 people/km²
Churches: P 43, C 5
Church per pop.: 1:19,219
Worship attendance: 932
Attendance/church: 22
Missionaries: 7

Geography

The northern part of Fukui consists of the Ono Basin and the Fukui Plain, with the Kuzuryu River running through the area. The southern area consists of Tsuruga Bay and a western lace-like shoreline. Complex mountain ranges run from the northeast to the southwest. The prefecture shares its border with Ishikawa, Gifu, Shiga, and Kyoto. A ragged shoreline in the northwest faces the Sea of Japan, creating a unique natural beauty which houses two national parks, the Kaga Coast and the Wakasa Bay. Due to the mountains and plains, this prefecture experiences heavy snow in winter and rain all year round, making the weather as complex as its geography.

Industry & Economy

The three Hokuriku prefectures, Fukui, Ishikawa and Toyama, are equally small, ranking lower than 30th in size. Despite its small size, Fukui as well as Toyama rank among the highest in rice production. The textile industry is equally strong. However, with a few exceptions, most are household centered small factories. Over 90% of the nation's eyeglass frames come from Sabae City. Traditional industries include Japanese paper manufacturing in Imadate.

Cultural Background

As with the others in the Hokuriku district, the people of Fukui are willing to endure difficulties and are generally positive about their present situation. They are friendly and kind to others. Possibly because of being close to the Kansai area, Fukui is more open to cultural change than the other two Hokuriku prefectures. However, many people hold on to old traditions and an emphasis on family ties.

Religious Milieu

There are more Buddhist temples per population in Fukui than any other prefecture in the nation. Echizen Yoshizaki was the base region for *Jodo Shinshu* Buddhist missions in the Hokuriku district and is located just inside Fukui prefecture on the Ishikawa border. The percent of Buddhists is the second highest in the nation next to Toyama, due in part to the Eiheiji Temple, headquarters of the Sodo sect founded by Dogen. Traditional Buddhist influence is so great that even Soka Gakkai has few believers here. Traditional festivals and activities also are an important part of community and home life.

The Mission

When the newer Buddhist sects came to Fukui they were strongly resisted. But the persistence of these early believers shows that it is possible to bring change even to this difficult area. Christians must be willing to sacrifice for the gospel as much as they did. During the Meiji era a brave missionary group from the Canadian Methodist Church brought the gospel here. Since the War era the Free Christian Mission from Norway has especially worked hard in Fukui. These testify to what hard work can do.

24 Pray that a Christian school can finally be started in Fukui. Pray for the teachers and children at the nine church-affiliated kindergartens.

25 Pray that Christian medical and welfare facilities may be established as a witness to the gospel. Pray for any Christian medical people that may be working here.

26 Pray that Christian training and camping facilities be established. Pray that God would raise up Christians who manage facilities that would be used for Christian ministry.

27 Pray for the ministry of Fukui Christian Book Store started by the Free Christian Ministry. Pray for radio programs aired by Fukui radio: *Light of Life* aired for five minutes daily, and *Beyond the Sunset* aired for 10 minutes every Sunday.

28 Pray that churches develop fellowship and cooperation that would build His Kingdom. Pray for pastors to be effective leaders of their flocks, and that there would be a strong sense of His Love throughout each fellowship.

Fukui is known for production of eyeglasses frames. Read Isaiah 29:18,19 and ask the Lord to open the spiritual eyes of the people of Fukui prefecture that they might be saved.

山梨 Yamanashi

Capital: Kofu
Population: 877,794
Cities: 7
  With 1 church: 2
Towns/Villages: 57
  With no churches: 40
  With 20,000 pop. &
  no churches: 0

Size: 4,254 km^2
Density: 206 people/km^2
Churches: P 61, C 5
Church per pop.: 1:14,390
Worship attendance: 1,448
Attendance/church: 24
Missionaries: 6

Geography

Yamanashi, an inland prefecture, straddles the *fosse magna* (great earth ditch) which divides Honshu Island into its eastern and western halves. On the east is the Kanto district and the west is the Southern Alps (the Akaishi Mountain Range). The central area, Kofu Basin, is sandwiched by Mount Yatsugatake to the north and Mount Fuji to the south. The east is isolated by the Misaka mountain terrain and the culture can be distinguished from that of the middle basin area. Weather in the basin area is very cold in the winter and hot in the summer. Snowfall is light and typhoon damage is infrequent.

Industry & Economy

Although rice production is relatively high, considering Yamanashi's land and weather conditions, its overall agricultural revenue is ranked low nationally due to the small cultivated acreage of rice fields and the low yield. Raising silk worms was once a thriving industry, but now Yamanashi ranks first in production of fruits, such as grapes and peaches. Yamanashi is not suitable for heavy industries, so light industries, such as textile and food processing, have taken the place of more traditional industries. In recent years, the resort industry has developed with the surrounding areas of Mounts Yatsugatake and Fuji becoming ideal vacation spots.

Cultural Background

After the Takeda family was defeated, no feudal lord resided in Yamanashi, and it was put under direct control of the Shogunate government. This historical background has created a unique culture. Also, mountains which surround most of the prefecture have forced people to have a strong sense of community. This sense of intimacy between family and friends is the strongest in the nation. On the other hand, as the expression "Merchants of Koshu" suggests, they are known for their attachment to their money.

Religious Milieu

The people of Yamanashi are neither particularly religious nor nonreligious. A well-loved quote by Shingen Takeda says, "People are the castle and the stone wall." In other words people are a better defense than a castle or stone wall. People here are more realistic, and visible factors are more important than the unseen. While completing his Buddhist training, Nichiren himself remained secluded in Minobu in the south. The Nichiren Buddhist headquarters were later established there. Even though the Aum Supreme Truth group had some of their facilities in Yamanashi while carrying out illegal activities, the people in the area were not involved in any way.

The Mission

The first outreach was undertaken by Methodist missionaries in 1877. Their activities included the starting of an English school (Yamanashi Eiwa Gakuin) and establishing lecture halls throughout Yamanashi. A number of denominations have churches in Kofu City, but rural villages have a very limited number of church facilities. With the modernizing of the railroad and highway connecting to Tokyo, people's attitudes are gradually changing. With the change we pray that this regional solidarity, described by Shingen as "stone walls" will soon open wider for the gospel.

29 Pray for the historic Christian school; Yamanashi Eiwa Gakuin School (girls' jr high/high and jr college at Kofu). Pray for Christian vocational schools: Nakayama Jissen Gakuin School (Kofu) and Fuji Culinary School (Fuji).

30 Pray for the social ministries at Donguri Ranch (Otsuki), Hosanna Garden (Fujiyoshida), Home of Light (Ichikawa Daimon).

31 Pray for Seisen Ryo Dormitory at the foot of Mount Yatsugatake. It was begun as the vision of Paul Rush to provide young people with hope, food and health.

1 Pray for these Christian retreat facilities: Japan Torchbearers Yamanakako Center, Tokyo YMCA Yamanakako Center, Zion Bible Camp (Lake Yamanaka), and several others.

2 Pray for Direction, the Christian book store in Kofu. Pray for *Gospel Time* aired on Yamanashi Radio. Pray for Yamanashi Church Conference meetings and ministry.

Yamanashi is where the headquarters of the strong Nichiren Buddhist sect are located as well as the infamous and defunct Aum Supreme Truth cult. Read Isaiah 44:9-11 and ask the Lord to bring low the religion of man and exalt His Son.

長野 Nagano

Capital: Nagano City	**Size:** 13,133 km²
Population: 2,190,307	**Density:** 167 people/km²
Cities: 17	**Churches:** P 151, C 19
With 1 church: 0	**Church per pop.:** 1:14,505
Towns/Villages: 103	**Worship attendance:** 3,250
With no churches: 76	**Attendance/church:** 22
With 20,000 pop. &	**Missionaries:** 71
no churches: 1	

Geography

Nagano prefecture sits in the center of the Japanese Islands. It is an inland prefecture 100 kilometers east to west and 200 kilometers north to south. It borders eight different prefectures and is the fourth largest prefecture. In the west are three mountain ranges running south to north, Hida, Kiso, and Akaishi, called the Japanese Alps. In the areas between these mountains are two valleys, Kiso with the Kiso River and Ina with the Tenryu river. The northeast area has many volcanoes. Here the Chikuma and Saikawa Rivers join and flow on to the Japan Sea as the Shinano River, creating the Saku and Nagano basins. In the center of the prefecture lie the Matsumoto and Suwa basins. Winters are rather cold, but precipitation is not that great and in the flat areas there is little snow damage.

Industry & Economy

Nagano prefecture is centered around agriculture with the highest percent of the population engaged in agriculture in the Kanto and Kinki areas. Because of the scarcity of flat land, production is small and barely ranks 10th in the nation. Production of rice and barley is limited, but lettuce and celery rank highest in the nation, with apples and grapes ranked second. Although it is not as thriving as it was in the past, the silk industry is still one of the main industries of the prefecture. The precision machinery industry in Suwa is a very promising industry which meets the challenging needs of a modern society.

Cultural Background

In ancient days Nagano was known as the Country of Shinano, where it was reported to have a large population and a high level of civilization. From the Sengoku era into the Edo era it was divided into smaller governmental divisions. Although it was finally reunified after many centuries, the Nagano prefecture is still characterized by many different local distinctives. Nagano is known as a prefecture of education, as demonstrated by the concern that parents have for their children's study.

Religious Milieu

Despite the fact that Zenkoji Temple is seen as the symbol of Nagano, it is surprising that more people do not believe in life after death than any other prefecture. Nevertheless, many people do rely on Buddhism and Shintoism to deal with their everyday lives. Their philosophy focuses on utilitarianism and secularism, yet an ancestry worship originating in animism is incorporated in their beliefs as well. Popular folklore beliefs, which trace back to the ancient Mountain religion, originated here in Takayama. These beliefs are still strong as seen in the Mount Fuji and Mount Ontake pilgrim associations.

Although there are several Christian medical facilities, there is only one Christian school, the Catholic Seisen Girls' High School and Jr College at Nagano City.

The Mission

In the early years of the Meiji era, missionaries and the returning residents who accepted Christianity started churches; first in Ueda in 1868, then in Nagano City, and major cities such as Matsumoto and Ina. Although the people of this prefecture are known to be very conservative, their steadfastness has and will become a vital key to the success of spreading the gospel. Karuizawa and Lake Nojiri have important summer resorts for missionaries. They have become excellent locations for the local residents to learn about Christianity.

3 Pray that Protestant schools be established. Also pray for the church-affiliated kindergartens in various areas.

4 Pray for the Christian medical facilities: San-iku-kai Toyono Hospital, Shinsei Hospital (Obuse) and its affiliated ministry for the elderly, and Aiwa Hospital (Nagano). Pray for other Christian physicians, and their witness.

5 Pray for Chaldea Kai Ueda Izumi Garden, a facility for the mentally disabled. Pray for Kobokan Kutsukake Children's Home (Karuizawa). Pray for church-affiliated nursery programs in various areas.

6 Pray for Christian camp and pension facilities: Megumi Chalet Karuizawa, Lake Matsubara Bible Camp, Tokyo YMCA Mount Nobeyama Center, Tokyo YMCA Nojiri Camp, Tokyo YWCA Nojiri Camp, and many other Christian facilities.

7 Pray for Christian book stores: Ueda Bible Center, Yutakana Inochi Bible (Matsumoto). Pray for radio programs: *The Light of The World* and *True Salvation* aired on Shin-etsu Radio.

Nagano is known as a prefecture of education. Read Ephesians 6:4 and ask the Lord to impress upon the Christians in this prefecture the importance of this verse.

June 8~12

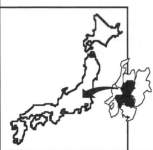

岐阜 Gifu

Capital: Gifu City
Population: 2,099,352
Cities: 14
  With no churches: 1
  With 1 church: 3
Towns/Villages: 85
  With no churches: 65
  With 20,000 pop. & no churches: 4

Size: 10,596 km^2
Density: 198 people/km^2
Churches: P 85, C 6
Church per pop.: 1:24,698
Worship attendance: 2,198
Attendance/church: 26
Missionaries: 15

Geography

Although Gifu is the nation's seventh largest prefecture, the percent of inhabitable land ranks second lowest in the nation (Kochi ranks the lowest). The southern district called Mino meets Aichi prefecture at the Nobi Plains. The northern district called Hida is centered around the small Takayama Basin which is surrounded by tall mountains of over 2,000 meters. The southern and northern regions draw contrasting pictures of geography as well as climate. The Mino district enjoys a relatively warm climate with many sunny days. The Hida district is typical of an inland mountain region with severe winter cold, heavy snowfall in the mountains and year-round rainfall.

Industry & Economy

The cultivated lands centered in the Mino district provide an area for rice and vegetable production. This district used to be plagued by rain disasters but now levees have greatly minimized the problem. Due to its vast forest and mountains, Hida has a thriving forestry industry. Since each district benefits from only one major industry, the overall economy of Gifu ranks neither high nor low in the national averages. As for the mining industry, the Kamioka area is known for lead and zinc production. There are not many large factories in the prefecture.

Cultural Background

During the Sengoku era, the Mino area was combined with Owari and Mikawa (now Aichi prefecture) and found itself in the midst of many power struggles. As a result, it has produced many famous wartime figures including Oda Nobunaga. Despite its colorful history, the people of Gifu are conservative and very content with their way of life. They are also very independent and hard working.

Religious Milieu

Gifu ranks fourth from the bottom on the national scale regarding the number of people who believe in life after death. As for the number of Buddhist believers Gifu ranks fourth from the top, following the three Hokuriku prefectures. Gifu is called the "money box" for *Jodo Shinshu* Honganji Temple, with its temples found throughout the prefecture. Traditional religious activities include the Takayama Festival, one of the nation's three main festivals, held every spring and fall. It also is the base for the international sanctuary of a fast-growing new religion called *Sukyo Mahikari*.

The Mission

Rev. Franson from Sweden had a strong burden for Japan, and established the Scandinavian Alliance Mission (now TEAM). They chose the Hida area for their missionary field because it was one of the most remote places in Japan. The resulting Domei Association celebrated its 100th anniversary in 1994 at Takayama with more than 1,000 attending. The convenience of present day transportation and modern communication development made it difficult to imagine the sacrifices of those early missionaries.

8 Pray for Gifu Seibi Gakuin (Seibi Girls' High School and Chubu Women's Jr College), the only Christian school in Gifu. Pray that a Christian school be started in the northern area and that a Christian boys' school also be established. Pray for the Christian teachers.

9 Pray for Gifu Kunmo (Training for the blind) Society whose facilities include a braille library and Aimo Hall. Also pray for the Japan Children's Foster Home in Gifu City. Pray that Christian medical facilities be established.

10 Pray for Christian retreat facilities: Abram's Inn (Kokufu), Nagoya YMCA Hiwada Kogen Camp (Takane), Neo Christian Sanso, and Sparrows Inn's Christian Hall (Ena).

11 There is no Christian book store in Gifu. Pray especially that people in the north have easier access to Christian literature. Pray for the TV program *Harvest Time*, and the radio programs, *Light of The World* and *Children of Star*.

12 Pray for Mino City (26,000) which has no church. Pray for the Gifu Christian Association and for fellowship and encouragement of the northern churches not a part of that group. Pray for the completion of the nursing home being planned in the north.

Gifu is one of the most spiritually depressed prefectures as far as impact of the gospel. Read Zephaniah 3:14-17 and ask the Lord to give assurance to His covenant people and allow them to experience His victory and pleasure in them.

静岡 **Shizuoka**

Capital: Shizuoka City	Size: 7,325 km^2
Population: 3,734,279	Density: 510 people/km^2
Cities: 21	Churches: P 227, C 27
With 1 church: 3	Church per pop.: 1:16,451
Towns/Villages: 53	Worship attendance: 6,655
With no churches: 23	Attendance/church: 29
With 20,000 pop. &	Missionaries: 33
no churches: 2	

Geography

Shizuoka is in the southeast part of the Chubu area with Hakone at the Kanagawa border. Mount Fuji rises at the Yamanashi border, and the Akaishi Mountain Range separates Shizuoka from Nagano. The Aichi border is marked by gentle hills. The *fosse magna* (great earth ditch) divides the prefecture into eastern and western halves. The eastern side consists of the Izu Peninsula and Suruga Bay, the west is made up of a simple shoreline, created by the Enshu Nada, stretching from Omaezaki to the Atsumi Peninsula. Hand-shaped Lake Hamana was once a gulf, but is now separated from the ocean by a sandbank. Weather is typical of the Pacific Ocean side, with mild temperatures and much rain. The area along the Enshu Nada is blessed with more clear days than anywhere else in the nation.

Industry & Economy

Due to its transportation systems, natural resources, and population, Shizuoka ranks in the top ten for its overall economy. Reflecting the industrial activity along the Tokaido Belt, manufacturing constantly ranks fifth to seventh in the nation. Developing industrial areas include the Hamamatsu area and the Suruga Bay shore area. Shizuoka is the national top producer of tea. Other produce includes melons grown in greenhouses, tangerine oranges, and strawberries. The fishing industry registers the 8th highest in tonnage of catch. They have the largest catch of tuna in the nation.

Cultural Background

In ancient days the Nakayama Trail following the ocean shore was the main means of transportation between east and west, mainly due to the geographic features of several large rivers and mountains which slope down to the shorelines. The opening of the Tokai Road enabled further development of rails and roads, which opened up an opportunity for Shizuoka to be influenced by both the Tokyo and Kansai culture. Urbanization of Shizuoka is certainly in progress. The Tokaido Development Project linking Tokyo to Osaka finds Shizuoka right in the middle.

Religious Milieu

Religious awareness among the people of Shizuoka is slightly below average, according to surveys. They show an interest in materialism, and do not strongly rely on the gods or Buddha. Neither do they rank high in valuing family status or tradition. Though they do not especially have close community relations, they are very friendly and relatively open toward the outside. The Fujinomiya Sengen Shrine in Fujinomiya, one of the ancient religious establishments, is the origin of Mount Fuji worship. This city also houses the Taisekiji Temple of Nichiren, connected with Soka Gakkai.

The Mission

The recent urbanization has weakened much of the binding influence of the communities and families, but it has also created an individualistic isolation. The increase in the number of churches is not keeping pace with the population increase in some areas, so there are many places that need new churches. The cities of Shizuoka and Mishima were main areas of missionary activity during the early years of the Meiji era, and Izu was an important target for the Alliance Mission. After the War, the Immanuel General Mission carried out extensive mission work in the prefecture and now has nine churches in the area.

13 Pray for the Christian schools: Shizuoka Eiwa Girls' School (jr/high schools, jr college), Shimizu International Jr High/High School, Seirei Gakuen (Christopher University of Nursing Science, Hamamatsu Jr College for Health, and its high school, Training School for Medical Care in Hamamatsu).

14 Pray for the Seirei Welfare medical work at Mikatagahara Hospital, Numazu Hospital, Hamamatsu Hospital, and the medical examination center. Also pray for the older Kamiyama Fukusei Hospital and the Ikuseikai Tokai Clinic (Hamaoka).

15 There are many welfare facilities here due to the good climate and accessibility. Pray for these welfare facilities: Musashinokai (Sakura and Fuji Gakuen at Gotemba) for the mentally disabled; Lake Hamana Garden of Eden (Hosoe) and Garden of The Cross (Gotemba, Izu Heights, and Hamamatsu) for the elderly, etc.

16 Pray for these Christian camping facilities: Tozanso (Gotemba), Amagi Sanso (Amagi Yugashima), Umegashima Lutheran Camp (Shizuoka), Lake Hamana Regal Gourd (Kosai), Hamana Fukuinso (Mikkabi), and others.

17 Pray for Christian book stores: Shizuoka Seibunsha, Life Centers at Shizuoka and Toyohashi, Hamamatsu Christian Book Store Ozora. Pray for *Life Line* and *Harvest Time* on TV and *Gospel Hour* aired on Shizuoka Radio.

Mount Fuji, the symbol of Japan's national/religious identity, is on Shizuoka's northern borders. Read Psalm 2:8 and ask the Father to exalt His Christ over the nation of Japan.

June 18~22

愛知 Aichi

Capital: Nagoya
Population: 6,770,293
Cities: 31
  With 1 church: 3
Towns/Villages: 57
  With no churches: 38
  With 20,000 pop. &
  no churches: 12

Size: 5,138 km^2
Density: 1,318 people/km^2
Churches: P 307, C 39
Church per pop.: 1:22,053
Worship attendance: 11,071
Attendance/church: 36
Missionaries: 85

Geography

Aichi is in the southwest part of the Chubu district. Eastern Aichi, Mikawa, occupies the southern tip of the Kiso mountain range, called the Mikawa Heights, with the Toyohashi Plain on the east and the Okazaki Plain on the west. Two peninsulas, Atsumi and Chita, extend from the coastline forming Mikawa bay. In the west the Owari district occupies the southern half of the Nobi Plain. Running through this plain are the Kiso, Nagara and Ibi Rivers, all eventually flow into the Bay of Ise, also forming borders with Gifu and Mie prefectures. The climate is generally mild with much rain. Winter brings very dry weather.

Industry & Economy

Aichi has the fourth largest population in the nation. With Nagoya midway between Tokyo and Osaka, it has become an economic and cultural force in Japan. Agriculture is a leading industry with a gross product that ranks sixth in the nation. Since the Edo era it has been called "The Vegetable Farming Kingdom," being the fourth highest vegetable producer in the nation. It ranks third in poultry and eggs. Next to Keihin and Hanshin, the Chukyo industrial district is the third largest of its kind and is the center of Aichi's manufacturing industry. This area is growing along the Bay of Ise toward Yokkaichi and also into the Chita Peninsula, expanding the chemical industry's national market share.

Cultural Background

Aichi's roots directly connect with the Tokugawa clan, with Mikawa noted as the clan's ancestral origin. One of the three Tokugawa brothers ruled from the Nagoya Castle on Owari, and it still bears a golden dolphin on the castle roof as a mark of that influence. Aichi was also a main juncture of the old Tokaido road. It now is marked by the Bullet Train tracks and the Tomei Express Highway. Despite the numerous historical events that make up Aichi's history, it is said that the people of Aichi feel alienated both socially and politically.

Religious Milieu

Many people of Aichi have feelings of uncertainty about life, possibly because of their bent towards realism. There are few traditional large-scale festivals in spite of the large number of Buddhists. The Toyokawa Inari Shrine is well known, and as a result of syncretism temple guardian gods have become objects of Shinto worship. The sword of the famous warrior, Yamatotakeru no Mikoto, called *Kusanagi no Tsurugi*, is kept in the Atsuta Shrine. During the War the popularity of the shrine was second only to the Ise Shrine. Many worshippers still gather here during New Year's.

The Mission

Even though the population is growing rapidly in the areas around Nagoya, the growth of churches is slow. These newly developed towns are relatively free from traditional religious and cultural restraints, and the residents tend to be spiritually thirsty. Several church and mission groups are targeting these areas, but there is a need for many more.

18 Pray for Christian schools: Kinjo Gakuin (girls' jr and high schools, women's jr college and college), Nagoya Gakuin (high school), Ryujo Women's Jr College, all in Nagoya, Nagoya Gakuin University in Seto; and YMCA/YWCA-affiliated vocational schools.

19 Pray for Christian medical facilities: Aichi International Hospital and its nursing care facility, Aisen Home, Agape Clinic, both in Nisshin, also for Itsugi Home for children in Inuyama.

20 Although there are many Christians in Aichi, many more Christian medical and welfare facilities could be started, providing an effective gospel witness. Ask the Lord to raise up people with that kind of vision.

21 Pray for the Christian book stores in Nagoya: CLC, Life Center and Seibunsha. Pray for radio programs: *Invitation to Christianity* and *Bible Stories* aired by Chubu Nippon Radio.

22 Pray for the fellowship and cooperation within the Tokai Mission Congress made up of church organizations in Nagoya and the surrounding areas. Pray for Tokai Bible Theological Institute, a nondenominational school, which trains local Christians for the ministry.

Aichi has 12 towns with over 20,000 people which have no churches, as well as 38 smaller villages with no churches. Read Habakkuk 2:14 and ask the Lord to begin a new work in these churchless cities, towns and villages.

Radio and TV

In Japan a privately owned radio station aired the nation's first broadcast in 1951, and in 1969 FM radio became available. The first television service in black and white began in 1953, and color television was launched in 1960, with UHF starting in 1968, and satellite broadcasting in 1990.

During the early stages of television, due to technical wave length frequencies, it did not have the radio's capability of worldwide broadcasting. When satellite broadcasting became available in 1963, people could instantaneously learn of events happening around the world. The importance of radio has not changed, but it has ceased to be a medium around which families would gather. Instead, it has become a private entertainment media.

As the role of the different mass media has changed, obviously programming has needed to be adapted. Now with the rapid spread of cable TV in Japan the church has a new opportunity at hand. And the importance of radio and television will continue to grow as a mass media tool for evangelism.

23 Pray for Pacific Broadcasting Association (PBA). It began airing *The Light of The World* in 1952 only one year after the nation's first radio broadcasting service was launched. PBA's production includes the TV program *Life Line* which is seen in most of Japan.

24 Pray for the Japan center of FEBC (Far East Broadcasting Co.), the largest Christian radio ministry in the world. Many Japanese programs for evangelism and Christian life are produced, and then broadcast back into Japan from FEBC stations abroad. Both medium and short wave bands are used.

25 Pray for Harvest Time Ministry. This weekly TV program has been broadcasting now for about ten years on 15 Japan stations and five U.S. It seeks to convey the love of God and His Son, the living Christ.

26 Pray for Christian Communications International. For a number of years the group broadcasted the Rex Humbard TV program throughout the nation. Although it is no longer available on TV, the ministry continues to follow up those touched by the programs.

99.1% of Japanese households have a color TV. (Japan Almanac, *1997, Asahi Shinbunsha*)

近畿 Kinki District

Population: 22,226,969
Cities: 102
  With no churches: 0
  With 1 church: 3
Towns/Villages: 293
  With no churches: 187
  With 20,000 pop. &
    no churches: 9

Size: 33,073 km^2
Density: 672 people/km^2
Churches: P 1,489, C 152
Church per pop.: 1:14,927
Worship attendance: 57,628
Attendance/church: 39
Attendance/pop.: 0.26
Missionaries: 369

Kinki district is half the size of the Chubu district but has about the same population. The Kanto district has the highest population density in Japan, followed by the Kinki (1/2). The population is centered around Kyoto, Osaka and Kobe, while many declining population communities can be found around the Kii Peninsula and the Chugoku mountain region. Until Tokyo became the capital city of Japan, the Kinki district was for more than 10 centuries the cultural center of the country. Kyoto once housed the Imperial Court. Osaka was the city of trade/commerce. Nara prefecture has been one of the more difficult areas for ministry due to the people's conservative nature. Surprisingly, during the past 10 years, more churches have been started in Nara than in any other prefecture in Kinki. This is due to Nara becoming an easy commute to Osaka, and to foreign missionaries seeing the need and concentrating their efforts in Nara. Any future effort should focus on the southern region of Shiga and the northern region of Mie where the population growth is exceeding the number of church plants. The Kinki Broadcast Ministry Association (*Kinpoden*) was founded in 1972, and has not only been effective in promoting the radio ministry, it has also been used to forge a strong cooperative spirit among Evangelical churches.

27 Several years ago a church was finally started in the difficult city of Tenri, at last establishing a church in each of the cities in the Kinki District. However, since Tenri has a population of 70,000, three more churches are needed to bring it to the national average. There are nine towns with a population of over 20,000 without a church. Eight of these are growing towns. Among these, over the past five years, the population of Komono, Mie has grown by 3,000, and Yumesaki, Hyogo by 2,000.

28 Many churches suffered damage in the 1995 Hanshin earthquake and have yet to fully recover. Church members died. Rebuilding has been very slow. Many members have had to leave the area for financial and work reasons. Pray for special strength and encouragement to move forward. Ask the Lord to provide needed funds and move in the hearts of other Christians to give their offerings to help.

三重 Mie

Capital: Tsu
Population: 1,843,869
Cities: 13
 With 1 church: 2
Towns/Villages: 56
 With no churches: 46
 With 20,000 pop.
  & no churches: 3

Size: 5,778 km²
Density: 319 people/km²
Churches: P 74 , C 11
Church per pop.: 1:24,917
Worship attendance: 2,362
Attendance/church: 32
Missionaries: 19

Geography

Mie is located in the southeastern area of the Kinki district. To the north the Yoro mountains form the border with Gifu prefecture, and the southern area meets Wakayama prefecture towards the bottom of the Kii Peninsula. This long narrow prefecture runs 175 kilometers from north to south. The eastern area faces Ise Bay and Kumano-Nada, and the western area meets Shiga and Nara prefectures. The distance between the eastern and western points is only 30-80 kilometers. The western side of Mie is very mountainous. In fact, the Ise Plain is the only flat land found in the prefecture, stretching from the northern region to the Shima Peninsula along Ise Bay. Weather is generally rather warm and humid. However, the southern Kii Peninsula experiences heavy rainfalls due to the Pacific Ocean influence.

Industry & Economy

Except for the heavy industries around Yokkaichi and Tsu, the whole area centers on agriculture and forestry. Although Mie has the second highest ratio of people engaged in agriculture in the Kinki and Tokai area, the gross agricultural product is not especially high. Mie does, however, enjoy good rice and vegetable crops, with tea leaves (third in the nation), rape seeds, sweet potatoes, radishes, and tangerines. Numerous privately owned forests provide a healthy forestry industry as well. A sound fishing industry and Mie's world famous cultured pearls are made possible by its excellent seaports.

Cultural Background

Sitting just beyond the mountains is the ancient city of Yamato (Nara) which played an important role in the cultural development of the prefecture. Yamato's influence can be seen in the Ise Shrine and early development of transportation systems, both land and sea. Commercial activities advanced quickly in spite of the necessity to use boats before an adequate land connection was developed between Tsu and Nagoya. Growth was advanced even further when the New Tokai Road opened between Suzuka and Kyoto.

Religious Milieu

The Ise Shrine has long been one of the most famous in Japan. It is here that the imperial ancestors are enshrined, making it the central place of worship. After the Meiji era the shrine was used to unify the nation around Shintoism. As a part of this movement, the shrine was given the exclusive right to sell certain religious paraphernalia, which has given it a solid financial base. Mie and Shiga prefectures have the highest percentage of Shinto believers in western Japan. There are also many Buddhist followers.

There are several Protestant and Catholic schools in the prefecture, but no medical facilities.

The Mission

In the late 16th century Ujisato Gamo, Lord of Matsuzaka, and other area leaders were baptized, influencing many to follow them. They were mainly located in the areas of Ise and Iga. Out of Japan's 26 saints who were martyred at Nagasaki in 1597, five were said to be from Ise. Ise Shrine is certainly a hindrance to evangelism, but because the people have had so many contacts with people who come to the shrine from all over Japan, they are generally open-minded and less conservative.

29 Pray for the Aino Gakuen Agricultural High School in Aoyama and the Holy Cross Welfare Vocational School in Komono.

30 Pray that Christian medical facilities be finally established. Pray for the Christian facilities for the elderly: Holy Cross Home in Komono and Suzuka, and King's Garden Mie in Kisei.

1 Pray for the ministry of Hakusan Agape Prayer Center. Pray that a Christian book store may be established so that people have an easier access to Christian publications without having to travel to Nagoya.

2 Pray for the Christian programs: *Harvest Time* televised by Mie Television and two radio programs sponsored by Shalom Promotion and aired by FM Mie.

3 Kameyama and Toba cities have only one church each, which puts them below the national church to population average. Pray that additional churches will be started especially in the areas around Kuwana and Tsu, where the population is growing significantly.

Mie is the home of Ise Shrine, the unifying link for the Shinto religion. Read Isaiah 49:24-26, and ask the Lord to break the stranglehold of this religion and set the captives free.

滋賀 Shiga

Capital: Otsu
Population: 1,283,341
Cities: 7
  With 1 church: 0
Towns/Villages: 43
  With no churches: 26
  With 20,000 pop.
    & no churches: 1

Size: 5,778 km^2
Density: 318 people/km^2
Churches: P 72 , C 7
Church per pop.: 1:17,824
Worship attendance: 1,909
Attendance/church: 27
Missionaries: 39

Geography

This inland prefecture occupies the northeastern region of the Kinki district, at the narrowest part of Honshu Island. The Omi Basin is in the middle of the prefecture surrounded by mountains and on the southeast is the Minakuchi Hills. Lake Biwa, Japan's largest lake, takes up 1/6 of the prefecture. The northern area meets Fukui prefecture at the Nosaka mountains, just ten kilometers from the Sea of Japan. The Sea of Japan brings extremely heavy winter snowfall to the northern part of Shiga. The south has a mild climate and sparse rainfall. Heavy rains occasionally cause Lake Biwa to flood.

Industry & Economy

Shiga's agricultural industry until recent years was stagnant, and suffered due to a decreasing population. But this is now turning around with the southern section becoming a suburb for those commuting to Kyoto and Osaka. The prefecture's rice has a good reputation. However, the number of full-time farmers is declining with more farmers engaging in alternative businesses. Statistics show that 3.8% of farmers are full timers (lowest in the nation) and that 92% have a second business (highest in the nation). Other specialty products include Omi beef, mosquito nets (highest producer in the nation), velvet, and Shigaraki ware. Growing industries include electronic and biotechnology related businesses.

Cultural Background

Shiga has a rich cultural background. It is close to the ancient capital of Kyoto, and Shiga itself for a brief time served as the capital of Japan. Surprisingly, old traditions and customs are valued less in Shiga than in any other prefecture. Perhaps the old values restrain the people's lives to the point where they feel as if they are suppressed. Omi merchants are known to be diligent, frugal, and honest, and many good business people come from Shiga.

Religious Milieu

Shiga has the third largest Buddhist population in the nation and many temples such as the Hieizan Enryakuji Temple, the head temple of the Tendai sect, one of the main schools of Buddhism. There are also many historic shrines such as the Taga and Hiyoshi Shrines. Participation in the traditional religious festivals is a strong part of family and community life.

The Mission

Oda Nobunaga, the first feudal lord to bring unity to the country in the 1500s, was initially friendly to the early Christian work. As a result, active missionary work took place around Azuchi, with many chapels and theological schools established. When the persecution began, it was also strong in that area. Aggressive pioneering efforts were made in the early years of the Meiji era and a number of churches were begun. After the War, WEC International (Worldwide Evangelization for Christ International) was able to establish 11 churches and preaching points throughout the prefecture. Now, as the population increases there is an increasing need and opportunity for aggressive evangelism.

4 Pray for the Christian schools: Omi Kyodai-sha School (jr and high schools in Omi Hachiman) founded by the Omi brothers and Seisen Jr College in Hikone. Intercede for the ministries of the church-affiliated kindergartens.

5 Pray for the Christian medical facilities: Vories Memorial Hospital named after the founder of Omi Brothers Co., and Omi Airin Home Imazu Hospital, and for their success in spreading the gospel. Also pray for Christians working in medical services throughout the prefecture.

6 Pray for the Christian welfare facilities: Shiyo Gakuen at Notogawa for the severely mentally disabled, Seiko Garden for the physically disabled and Seifu Home for the elderly (both at the same site in Imazu).

7 Pray for the Christian camping facilities: Kosai Home for Prayer (Jesus Christ Church in Japan at Shin Asahi); Oku Biwa-ko Camp (Japan Holiness Church at Nishi Azai); WEC Shinsei Camp (Omi Hachiman).

8 There are no Christian book stores at all. Pray for the Christian TV programs: *Life Line* and *Harvest Time* aired on Lake Biwa Broadcasting. Pray for good cooperation and fellowship through groups such as the Ashram Center and the Shiga Interdenominational Pastors Fellowship.

Shiga's people value old traditions and customs less than other prefectures in Japan. Read Colossians 4:5-6 and ask the Lord to stir up the Christians in Shiga to make the most of this opportunity.

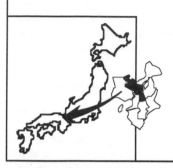

京都 **Kyoto**

Capital: Kyoto City
Population: 2,551,061
Cities: 11
  With 1 church: 0
Towns/Villages: 33
  With no churches: 22
  With 20,000 pop.
  & no churches: 0

Size: 4,613 km^2
Density: 553 people/km^2
Churches: P 203, C 33
Church per pop.: 1:12,567
Worship attendance: 7,144
Attendance/church: 35
Missionaries: 57

Geography

Kyoto, in the northern area of the Kinki district, faces the Japan Sea on the north. Northern Kyoto is the only part of Kyoto not surrounded by mountains. The east is bordered by Fukui and Shiga prefectures and the Hira and Tamba Mountains. On the west is Hyogo prefecture and the Tango and Chugoku Mountain Ranges. At the south border is Osaka and Nara. All of Kyoto is an intricate land formation that has created a series of small basins. One such basin is the Kyoto Basin. That area and to the south experience large temperature fluctuations from summer to winter. The north has heavy winter snowfalls.

Industry & Economy

Kyoto, the old capital of Japan, draws millions of tourists every year. Because of the many mountains, agriculture has never been strong here. The one exception is tea; Kyoto and Nara are always in competition for 4th or 5th position in the nation. Uji Tea is especially well-known for its quality. Sake and the well-known Fushimi Sake is also profitable, ranking among the best in the nation. There are still numerous traditional industries such as Nishijin weaving, Yuzen dyeing, Kiyomizu pottery and Tango silk. Most of these operate as small, family-sized factories. There are new industrial developments centered around Maizuru Bay and the expanding Hanshin Industrial District.

Cultural Background

The traditions established during the Heian era have been a source of pride for Kyoto. Although *heian* means "tranquil and peaceful," Kyoto has had more than its share of struggles, revolutions, and wars. Perhaps this historical background has influenced the thinking of the people of Kyoto. Able to blend both traditional and modern thinking, the people are conservative while demonstrating a political preference that can be classified as reformist.

Religious Milieu

Kyoto is full of temples and shrines. Kyoto and Nara have long been leading centers for Buddhist activities. Of those Buddhist groups whose activities cover more than one prefecture, nearly 40 have their headquarters in Kyoto. However, it is surprising to note that the percentage of Buddhists is about half that of Toyama and Ishikawa prefectures. Before the War a new religion called Omotokyo was begun by Deguchi at Kameoka. Although it encountered severe oppression, the sect eventually established its temple at Ayabe.

The Mission

In the late 1500s Catholic Christianity spread through Kyoto and its surrounding areas, and at the peak of the movement the church was even stronger in Kyoto than in Kyushu. And yet in the early years of the Meiji era the Protestant work encountered heavy Buddhist resistance. The beginning of Doshisha English School by Jo Niishima helped to open the door for different groups to come and start more churches. During the prewar period Kyoto churches made important contributions to the national Christian activities. This continued after the War, with the first two Japan Congresses on Evangelism sponsored by the Japan Evangelical Association being held in Kyoto.

9 Pray for Christian educational establishments: Doshisha (college, women's jr college and college, jr high and high schools, girls' jr high and high schools, Kori Jr High School, international jr high and high schools), Heian Women's Schools (jr college, jr high and high schools), and Kyoto YMCA International Vocational School.

10 Pray for Christian medical facilities: Japan Baptist Hospital; its nursing school and facility for the elderly and Saeki Obstetrics and Gynecology Clinic.

11 Pray for Christian welfare facilities: Aiikushin'en Hope Home for Mothers-Children, Maizuru Futaba Home for children; facilities for the mentally disabled; Shirakawa School for the mentally disabled, Hinadori School, and Doho Home in Uji.

12 Pray for the ministries of: Japan Christian Academy Kansai Seminar House, Kyoto YMCA Retreat Center, CLC Books Kyoto Store, Jordan Co. Kyoto Branch Store, The Gospel House KYOTO.

13 Pray for Christian media programs: *Harvest Time* televised on KBS Kyoto and the radio program, *Miraculous Counselor*. Pray that the churches in Kyoto may be based on an evangelical understanding of the gospel and that they may be united in fellowship and cooperation.

Kyoto was established as the capital of Japan during the Heian (peace and tranquillity) period. Read Romans 5:1 and ask the Lord to reveal His true peace through Jesus Christ.

大阪 Osaka

Capital: Osaka
Population: 8,592,991
Cities: 33
 With 1 church: 0
Towns/Villages: 11
 With no churches: 5
 With 20,000 pop. &
  no churches: 1

Size: 1,868 km²
Density: 4,600 people/km²
Churches: P 558, C 45
Church per pop.: 1:15,400
Worship attendance: 25,143
Attendance/church: 45
Missionaries: 93

Geography

Osaka prefecture occupies the center of the Kinki district. It has mountains on three sides with the west side facing Osaka Bay. Kyoto and Hyogo meet Osaka's north border at the Tamba mountain range. On the east it borders Nara at the Ikoma and Kongo mountain ranges. Wakayama and the Izumi mountain range form the west border. The Osaka Plain, Kinki's largest plain, lies toward the center and the north. Osaka has a very mild climate, mostly due to the influence of the Inland Sea which makes for little rainfall and little variance in temperature.

Industry & Economy

Since medieval times Osaka has been built on commerce. The percentage of people engaging in agriculture is second lowest in the nation. Osaka's agricultural industry is minimal with the exception of vegetables to supply the Osaka metropolitan areas. The livestock industry is declining, but the food processing industry is rising. The Hanshin Industrial District along Osaka Bay with its heavy industry is further expanding to the Senshu areas. That is where the Kansai New International Airport was built, providing the area with tremendous growth potential. Other developing areas include extensive residential developments such as the Senboku New Town.

Cultural Background

At the time of the Meiji Restoration, Osaka and Tokyo were both prime candidates to replace Kyoto as Japan's new capital. The two cities have contrasting cultural backgrounds. Tokyo was based on the "samurai" culture, whereas Osaka had a "merchant" mentality. The latter culture has resulted in a way of life that emphasizes present benefits and realism. Although known for their skill in bartering, they do not hesitate to spend money on items they value.

Religious Milieu

The percentage of Buddhist believers is higher here than in either Kyoto or Hyogo. However, the number of people saying that they depend on religion for spiritual support is the second lowest in the nation. Folklore practices and festivals such as "Tokaebisu" and "Tenjin Festival," *Hokora* (a small rock altar) and *Yashikigami* (an altar for the household god) are constant reminders of the deep rooted religious traditions. A newer religion, PL Kyodan (Perfect Liberty), has its headquarters in Tondabayashi.

The Mission

Because of the Ishiyama Honganji Temple's strong religious control over Osaka, Christianity did not spread much during the *Kirishitan* era. Yet, the international port city of Sakai provided an excellent opportunity for ministry. Many famous stories originated in this city: The martyrdom of Mrs. Galatia Hosokawa took place here. Sen-no-Rikyu was from Sakai and some believe his famous tea ceremony was based upon Christian philosophy. Now Osaka is said to be more international than Tokyo, a fact which should influence the spread of the gospel here.

14 Pray for Christian schools: Baika Gakuen (women's college, jr college, jr high and high schools), Poole Gakuin (women's jr college, jr high and high schools), Osaka Women's Gakuin (jr college, jr high and high schools), Momoyama Gakuin (college, high school), Osaka Christian Gakuin (jr college), and Seikyo Gakuen (jr high and high schools).

15 Pray for Christian medical facilities: Aizomebashi Hospital, Kodokai Hospital, Galatia Hospital in Mino, Yodogawa Christian Hospital, Osaka Gyomeikan Hospital, Miyamoto Memorial Hospital, Christian Mead Social Welfare Center, and other Christian clinics/hospitals.

16 Pray for the many Christian welfare facilities: Salvation Army working with mothers and children, Osaka Saijo Rinpo Kan working with children and the elderly, and the Kamagasaki Christian Kyoyu Kai ministering to the underprivileged.

17 Pray for Christian retreat centers: Kansai Seikan, Lutheran Training Center, both at Nose, and Hotel The Luther. Also pray for Christian book stores: Osaka Life Center, Osaka Christian Book Stores, and others.

18 Pray for the Christian programs: *Life Line* televised on Sun Television, and various radio programs aired on Mainichi Radio, Asahi Radio and Radio Kansai. Pray for good fellowship and cooperation among Osaka Mission Prayer Meetings and other pastors' fellowships throughout the area.

Osaka is the second largest city/area in Japan. Read Psalm 67:1-3 and ask the Lord to make the 558 churches here a great blessing to the whole nation.

Areas Without Churches (1996)

How many people are living in areas without churches? The following statistics are calculated by taking the population of cities that have no churches plus the unchurched counties (*gun*). Since it does not include the towns and villages within the counties that have no churches, the percent is actually much higher. The first figure is the total unchurched population, and the second is the percent of the total population.

	Population	%		Population	%
Japan	**4,851,604**	**3.9**	Shiga	118,747	9.3
Hokkaido Total	**1,475,495**	**26.0**	Kyoto	74,765	2.9
Aomori	61,316	4.1	Osaka	16,458	0.2
Iwate	180,983	12.7	Hyogo	114,200	2.1
Miyagi	54,550	2.4	Nara	2,028	0.1
Akita	49,985	4.1	Wakayama	0	0.0
Yamagata	148,820	11.9	**Kinki District**	**597,236**	**2.7**
Fukushima	7,540	0.4	Tottori	0	0.0
Tohoku District	**503,194**	**5.1**	Shimane	47,438	6.1
Ibaraki	112,855	3.8	Okayama	119,208	6.1
Tochigi	44,535	2.3	Hiroshima	177,303	6.2
Gumma	46,808	2.3	Yamaguchi	35,378	2.3
Saitama	0	0.0	**Chugoku District**	**379,327**	**4.9**
Chiba	45,093	0.8	Tokushima	40,089	4.8
Tokyo	0	0.0	Kagawa	0	0.0
Kanagawa	0	0.0	Ehime	0	0.0
Kanto District	**249,291**	**0.6**	Kochi	47,659	5.8
Niigata	127,440	5.1	**Shikoku District**	**87,748**	**2.1**
Toyama	104,293	9.3	Fukuoka	140,339	2.9
Ishikawa	59,390	5.1	Saga	180,255	20.4
Fukui	31,647	3.8	Nagasaki	100,428	6.5
Yamanashi	0	0.0	Kumamoto	152,360	8.2
Nagano	45,452	2.1	Oita	73,982	6.0
Gifu	126,770	6.0	Miyazaki	143,582	12.1
Shizuoka	10,669	0.3	Kagoshima	101,494	5.7
Aichi	137,701	2.0	Okinawa	23,511	1.8
Chubu District	**643,362**	**3.0**	**Kyushu District**	**915,951**	**6.2**
Mie	271,038	14.7			

19 Every year many church-sponsored summer programs take place. These programs include family/children/youth camps, revival meetings, training camps, etc. Pray that these programs take place without any accidents. Pray that capable counselors/leaders may be led by the Holy Spirit to effectively share Jesus with the youth and children's groups.

20 SEA DAY
Today is set aside as a day to remember the ocean waters. Pray that this holiday will provided time for Christians to share the gospel. Pray for the safety and salvation of those engaged in marine industry including seamen, fishermen and others.

21 Pray for Operation Mobilization and its division here, OM Japan, as it sends out short-term missionaries from around the world to share the gospel throughout the world. Their ocean travel ministry is carried on by the staff of the Doulos and Logos II ships.

22 Pray for the Missionary Training Center (MTC) as it seeks to train Japanese and other Asians to become effective missionaries around the world.

23 Pray for *Kaigai Senkyo Renraku Kyoryokukai* (JOMA) and its work. It was founded to bring evangelical mission agencies together for encouragement and cooperation. Pray that many more Japanese missionaries be led to bring the gospel to other countries.

24 An increasing number of Japanese are working abroad. It is often very difficult for the children to fit into the culture when they come back to Japan. Pray for the children of Christian families that their international experience will be a positive thing for God's Kingdom; for the other children also that they will be more open to the gospel as they return.

25 More Japanese travel within Japan and internationally during these summer holidays than any other time of the year. Pray for safety in travel, and for thousands of divinely orchestrated happenings that will have eternal significance. Also pray for Christians who will meet Japanese on their trips, that they will be able to share the gospel.

26 There are many Christians who have been saved and baptized, but for a variety of reasons have not attended church for a long time. Pray that their faith be revived and that they return to their churches.

兵庫 **Hyogo**

Capital: Kobe
Population: 5,422,446
Cities: 21
  With 1 church: 0
Towns/Villages: 70
  With no churches: 41
  With 20,000 pop. &
  no churches: 4

Size: 8,381 km^2
Density: 647 people/km^2
Churches: P 422, C 36
Church per pop.: 1:12,849
Worship attendance: 36,593
Attendance/church: 40
Missionaries: 151

Geography

Hyogo occupies the northeastern region of the Kinki district, facing both the Sea of Japan and the Seto Inland Sea. The island of Awaji, located across the Akashi Strait, belongs to Hyogo. On the east is Kyoto and Osaka, and the west Tottori and Okayama. The Chugoku mountain range extends to the Tamba Highland, forming the watershed which divides the prefecture into north and south. Although the northern half which faces the Sea of Japan has no flat areas, the southern half is blessed with the Harima Plain. The southeastern region is a complex land formation which caused the Great Hanshin Awaji Earthquake of 1995. The weather is fairly temperate, though the north experiences heavy rainfall and severe winter snows.

Industry & Economy

Due to the large population of Kobe, both the gross agricultural product and those involved in farming amount to only 3%. However, Hyogo's total agricultural income is still above the national average. Leading products include onions (the nation's second highest) and products such as sake, and the world famous Kobe beef. Hyogo also has thriving steel and shipbuilding industries. Thanks to the various high quality mines, the mining industry is also healthy.

Cultural Background

Kobe, along with Yokohama, has a long history as an international port, allowing many foreign influences to be assimilated into the culture. The Meiji government's push towards modernization, foreign ships frequently docking there, and the many foreigners living in the area greatly accelerated the area's internationalization. Despite this, rural Hyogo is filled with communities still bound by old traditions and folklore beliefs.

Religious Milieu

Despite the area's historical background, Hyogo does not possess many famous shrines and temples. The Minatogawa and Ikuta Shrines in Kobe are more noteworthy examples. More than organized religion it is the traditional folklore, mixed with Buddhism and Shintoism that are deeply rooted in the people's lives. As for Christianity, after the ban was lifted, many foreign missionaries came to Hyogo and began establishing churches and mission schools. This is evident in the numerous churches seen in Kobe. There are also several theological schools in the Hyogo prefecture.

The Mission

In January, 1995, a great earthquake hit Kobe and the southern part of Hyogo prefecture, bringing mammoth destruction to the prefecture. Kobe had one of the highest ratios of church to population in the nation, and a number of these church buildings were damaged or demolished. The earthquake has done much to create a more positive Christian image, because of the resulting Christian relief ministry that is still going on.

27 Pray for Christian schools: Kobe Women's College, Shukugawa Gakuin Women's Jr College, Seiwa Jr College and College, Koei Preschool Education Gakuin, Kansai Gakuin University, Shoin Women's College, Hinomoto Women's Jr College, Keimei Girls' High School, Yatsushiro Gakuin University, and others.

28 Pray for the Christian medical facilities: Palmore Hospital, Kobe Adventist Hospital, Agape Kabutoyama Hospital, Kobe Kaisai Hospital, Oguni Hospital at Himeji, and others.

29 Pray for Christian welfare facilities: Jesus Dan, Seirei Welfare Jigyodan, and others. Pray for Christian book stores: Covenant, Kobe Christian, Nishinomiya Seibun, and for their ministry as they recover from the earthquake.

30 Pray for Christian retreat/camping facilities: Nosegawa Bible Camp, Osaka YMCA Rokko Retreat Center, Kansai Gakuin Sengari Seminar House, United Baptist Inagawa Camp, Kobe YMCA Hotel, Aogaki Camp, and others.

31 Pray for a quick recovery from the devastation of the earthquake, that church buildings may be reconstructed as soon as possible and that a city-wide redevelopment plan may be Christian-friendly. Pray for good fellowship and cooperation among the Kobe Missions Association and the prayer meetings by pastors and their spouses in western Kobe.

Hyogo was the site of the Great Hanshin earthquake in 1995. In the midst of the destruction, the Lord has brought a resurrection to the church. Read John 17:20-23 and ask the Lord to continue to draw the saints in this prefecture together in Christian love, service and witness.

奈良 Nara

Capital: Nara City	**Size:** 3,692 km²
Population: 1,434,579	**Density:** 389 people/km²
Cities: 10	**Churches:** P 89, C 8
With 1 church: 1	**Church per pop.:** 1:16,119
Towns/Villages: 37	**Worship attendance:** 2,606
With no churches: 23	**Attendance/church:** 29
With 20,000 pop. &	**Missionaries:** 61
no churches: 0	

Geography

This inland prefecture faces Mie on the east, Kyoto on the north, Osaka on the west, and Wakayama on the southwest. The Nara Basin occupying the northern half of the prefecture is the only flat land, and provides a home for the majority of its population and industry. To the south of the Yoshino River stands the Kii mountain range with Hachikenzan as the highest peak in the Kinki district. The narrow valleys snaking through these mountains are called "the solitary islands of land," hindering the development of an adequate transportation system. The basin area has very little rainfall and a wide range of seasonal temperatures. The mountain areas are relatively warm and rainy, especially Mount Odaigahara, which experiences the nation's highest precipitation, over 4,000 mm annually.

Industry & Economy

Nara is a relatively small prefecture with the fourth lowest amount of cultivated areas and the least amount of habitable land in the nation. Forests occupy 80% of the land. The most famous trees are the Yoshino cedars, well known for their quality. The Nara Basin produces much rice and fruit, and is the second in the nation for persimmons and fourth in tea. One specialty is the gold fish from Yamato, providing over half of the nation's supply. Due to the lack of land, manufacturing has been slow to develop.

Cultural Background

Nara served as the nation's capital twice, during the Asuka and then the Heijo era. Rarely visited by natural disasters, Nara had more opportunity for cultural development. This highly developed culture has been a source of pride for the prefecture. Even the remote mountainous areas of Yoshino and Kumano are mentioned in the myth in which Ninigi no Mikoto (grandson of Amaterasu Omikami, the goddess of the Sun) descended, and also in the story of the Period of Northern and Southern Dynasties.

Religious Milieu

There are numerous historic temples and shrines in Nara whose festivals can be traced back to ancient times. The high peak of Mount Omine is considered one of the sacred places of mountain asceticism. The city of Tenri was named after the Tenri religion (founded by Miki Nakayama at the end of the Tokugawa era) whose headquarters were established there. An awareness survey does not indicate a strong interest in religion, but it does reveal that the percentage of people who believe in life after death is the second highest in the nation.

The Mission

Although Nara prefecture has been a major center for non-Christian religion, it has produced many Christians such as Ukon Takayama and his son who were influenced by a Christian converted from mountain asceticism. After the Meiji era Japanese Christians and foreign missionaries aggressively pursued their mission and established churches despite hardships and obstacles. The postwar mission work has even reached into Tenri City. A number of new churches are being started around Ikoma, a commuter town outside Osaka.

1 Pray that the Nara YMCA Cram School may wisely demonstrate the gospel to the students. Although there are many Christian schools in the Hanshin district, Nara has no Christian colleges or high schools.

2 There are no Christian medical or welfare facilities, with the exception of one Catholic nursing home. Pray that many children will come to know Jesus in the church-affiliated preschools.

3 There are no Christian book stores in the prefecture. Pray for *Life Line* and *Harvest Time* shown on Nara Television.

4 Most of the villages and towns located in the eastern and southern regions with declining population are without churches, especially the vast southern region between the Yoshino and Totsu Rivers which is home to 80,000 people. Pray that God will raise up church planters with a vision for this area.

5 Pray for the newer and smaller churches which labor within a hard traditional environment. Also for missionary work around the rapidly growing areas.

Nara is the center of several major non-Christian religions. Read I John 5:18-21 and pray that the believers in Nara will take great encouragement from their position in Christ and that they will keep themselves from the influences of the world.

August 6~10

和歌山 **Wakayama**

Capital: Wakayama City
Population: 1,098,682
Cities: 7
   With 1 church: 0
Towns/Villages: 43
   With no churches: 23
   With 20,000 pop. &
    no churches: 0

Size: 4,725 km²
Density: 233 people/km²
Churches: P 71, C 12
Church per pop.: 1:15,474
Worship attendance: 1,787
Attendance/church: 25
Missionaries: 8

Geography

Wakayama occupies the southwest area of the Kii Peninsula. On the north is Osaka, the east Nara and Mie, with the rest of the prefecture facing the Pacific Ocean. Except for the area around the lower Kinokawa River, Wakayama has little flat area. The valley sandwiched between the Izumi mountain range at the Osaka border, and the Kinokawa River extends all the way to the Yoshino River in Shikoku. In the south there are numerous valleys running east and west. Weather generally is warm with heavy rainfall. The Kinokawa River area's climate is typical of that found by the Inland Sea.

Industry & Economy

Forests occupy approximately 80% of the prefecture, similar to Nara. Agriculture is weak here due to the lack of farming and habitable land. As a result many people, especially from the south, emigrated to the United States and Canada. Fruit growing is a thriving industry, and Wakayama is the nation's top producer of tangerines, plums, and persimmons. In spite of the long coast line, a lack of good fishing ports has limited the fishing industry. The steel industry had been a major part of the prefecture's economy until the major steel company at Wakayama City was relocated.

Cultural Background

Wakayama is known to be the most conservative prefecture in the Kinki district. It was once ruled by Lord Kishu, from one of the three Tokugawa families. The people still practice the traditional community system called *miyaza*, wherein families are closely tied to local temples. Generally speaking, the people of the Kinki district are relatively relaxed in their morals, but the people of Wakayama are quite conservative.

100

Religious Milieu

Kumano Shrine is a well known shrine dedicated to the god Kumano Gongen around the 3rd century by a group of people who immigrated here from the Izumo Country. It became the principal Kumano shrine for the whole nation. Kumano Gongen was later linked to the Mountain Religion. In the middle ages, as so often happened, the Tendai priests and priest-soldiers ruled Wakayama with a combination of Buddhism and Shintoism. Mount Koya in the northern part of the prefecture is known as a sacred place of the Shingon sect founded by Kobo Daishi.

The Mission

The people in south Wakayama appear relatively open-minded, even to the point of allowing a number of people to emigrate to foreign lands. However this has not led to an openness to Christianity. At the beginning of the Meiji era the ministry of the Hail brothers planted seeds that have had a broad influence for the gospel. Their work has been continued by the Japan Evangelistic Band. Also, after the War the Baptist General Conference came to Wakayama and has planted a number of churches along the coast.

6 There is only one Christian school here, a Catholic women's jr college. Pray that a Protestant school can also be established. Please remember Christian teachers working in secular schools.

7 Pray for the Ai no Sono Clinic (Kami Tonda), work of the Shin'ai Group, a social welfare foundation. Also pray that more Christian welfare facilities may be established. Pray that many resorts may provide possibilities for spreading the gospel.

8 Pray that Christian retreat/camp facilities may be constructed. Pray for Kohitsuji Book Store (Iwade), the only Christian book store in Wakayama. Christians throughout the area need easier access to Christian literature.

9 Pray for *Harvest Time* televised by Wakayama Television. Pray that radio programs may also become available.

10 Pray for a sense of unity and cooperation among the Christians, and for the Wakayama Pastor's Association. Pray that the gospel may reach towns and villages around Mount Koya and other mountainous areas where there are presently no churches.

Wakayama is known for its fruit production. Read Galatians 5:22-23 and ask the Lord to pour out His grace so that the churches in this prefecture may be known for the fruit of His Spirit.

中国 Chugoku District

Population: 7,763,515	Size: 31,785 km^2
Cities: 49	Density: 244 people/km^2
With no churches: 0	Churches: P 504, C 48
With 1 church: 7	Church per pop.: 1:15,404
Towns/Villages: 269	Worship attendance: 12,631
With no churches: 198	Attendance/church: 25
With 20,000 pop. &	Attendance/pop.: 0.16
no churches: 3	Missionaries: 63

Chugoku district has two distinct sides, the San'yo (Pacific Ocean side) and San'in (Sea of Japan side). San'yo population is growing, while the other side is decreasing. Tottori on the San'in side with no population growth has one of the best church per population ratios (13,462), while Hiroshima on the San'yo side with fast population growth has the least in Chugoku (17,190).

The overall district growth rate of churches in the past ten years is 11%, lowest in the nation, but because of population decline, the church per population ratio is improving. Actually, the truth is that in the past ten years the number of churches increased only by 51, making the total 504. There has been no significant improvement in the number of villages and towns without churches. Also, the populations of Hiroshima and Okayama will continue to grow. So both sides of the district need new evangelistic thrusts.

11 More churches are needed here! Pray that at least 50 churches out of the 504 will accept the challenge to start one other church in the next five years. The immediate need is for the cities of Hiroshima and Okayama with their population growth. Prayer is also needed for those individuals, groups, and churches making every effort in the ministry to the depleting mountain communities and to the establishment of the first churches there. The Inland Sea areas are also in need of the gospel.

12 Peace has been a leading concern for the people in the Chugoku district due to the fact that Hiroshima was a victim of the atomic bombing. May the peace brought by Jesus Christ be given to every individual of the Chugoku district! This peace can never be destroyed. Also, pray that the *Chugoku Chiho Senkyo no Tsudoi* (Chugoku District Missions Fellowship) stimulates good fellowship and cooperation among the churches.

Remembering WWII

On August 14, 1945, Japan accepted the Potsdam Proclamation and surrendered unconditionally, ending the Pacific Ocean side of World War II. It also brought closure to the three-year-long Greater East Asia fighting, the eight-year Sino-Japanese War, and the 15-year invasion of the Chinese continent by the Japanese military. It brought an end to 50 years of colonial rule in Taiwan, and to 35 years of cruel treatment to the people of Korea. On May 3, 1947, Japan was given a new constitution. For the next six years and eight months Japan was, for the first time ever, under the control of a foreign power. August 15th has been set aside to observe the ending of World War II. The phrase, "ending of a war," gives the impression that the war ended by itself. That is not true. A war never ends by itself. We Japanese must never forget our responsibility in beginning the war, and our defeat in the war. The same is true with Jesus. Unless we unconditionally accept the truth that we are sinners, true salvation and peace through Jesus Christ will never come.

13 Pray for *Inochi no Mizu Keikaku* (Water of Life Plan), a support organization for the Chinese underground churches. For 20 years China suffered from Japanese invasion and rule, and then from the oppression of communism. This support group provides Bibles for the underground church (house churches).

14 Pray for the ministry of OMF International. This organization was originally China Inland Mission (CIM) founded by Hudson Taylor. The group sends missionaries throughout Asia, and a number of Japanese missionaries are also part of the work. In Japan OMF has 128 missionaries, mostly active in church planting,

15 WWII COMMEMORATION DAY
Pray for South Korea, which suffered 35 years of harsh Japanese rule, and today bears the burden of the North-South division. Pray for the *Nikkan Shinzen Senkyo Kyoryoku Kai* (Japan-South Korean Good-Will Mission Association). It seeks to promote peaceful relationships between the two countries, sending and receiving missionaries and evangelistic ministries.

16 Pray for the Christian Gospel Mission Association, whose work includes ministry in China, former USSR nations, and other communist countries. Also pray for ministry efforts using Taiwan as a base to minister in China, Siberia, Mongolia and North Korea.

鳥取 Tottori

Capital: Tottori City
Population: 619,238
Cities: 4
   With 1 church: 0
Towns/Villages: 35
   With no churches: 26
   With 20,000 pop. &
   no churches: 0

Size: 3,494 km^2
Density: 177 people/km^2
Churches: P 46 , C 4
Church per pop.: 1:13,462
Worship attendance: 989
Attendance/church: 22
Missionaries: 2

Geography

Tottori faces the Sea of Japan on the north. In the south, Tottori meets Okayama at the Chugoku mountain range, while on the east is Hyogo and the west is Shimane. Tottori's total area is very small and is the nation's least populated prefecture. Towards the north are a number of volcanoes and in the east are three smaller plains, Tottori, Kurayoshi and Yonago. Along the shoreline are stretches of beautiful sandy beaches and sand dunes. Summers bring heavy rainfalls, and winters offer few sunny days and heavy snowfalls.

Industry & Economy

Due to its small population Tottori has the lowest gross agricultural production in the nation. Although the percentage of farmers is very high, production is low due to cold weather and a lack of flat lands. It does lead the nation in pears and is fourth in watermelons. With its excellent seaports Tottori has the biggest fishing haul among the prefectures on the Sea of Japan side, and is fourth in the nation. Uranium is mined around the Ningyo Pass located in the southern part of the prefecture.

Cultural Background

A large number of people, mainly metal work craftsmen from Korea, came to Tottori hundreds of years ago to cash in on metallic sands. This made Tottori quite progressive in its outlook. Until the Edo era the ocean was the main means of transportation, making port towns such as Sakai and Tottori cultural centers. These became less important once road and railway systems were developed. Now the area is often referred to as *Ura Nihon* (Japan's back side). The people of Tottori are known to be very conservative with tight-knit communities.

Religious Milieu

Tottori prefecture has a higher percentage of Buddhist followers than any other prefecture in the Chugoku district except Hiroshima, and the least percent of Christians. Although Buddhists were active in Tottori as early as the Nara era, only a few of the old temples remain. Among them are the ruins of Kokubunji at Kurayoshi and Saiono in the outskirts. Daisen established a monastery around the 8th - 9th century as the sacred headquarters of mountain asceticism and this still remains. There are no records of *Kirishitan* in the area, but it is believed that there were a number of converts. When Christianity became illegal, imprisoned Christians were treated relatively fairly by the lord, but later the Christians exiled from Uragami and Nagasaki were treated very cruelly.

The Mission

In the early years of the Meiji era missionaries were able to establish churches in the cities of Kurayoshi, Tottori, and Yonago. In the later years of the Meiji era, Toyo Senkyokai (later renamed Holiness) actively ministered in Yonago. The ministry was launched by the famous missionary, B.F. Buxton, headquartered in Matsue, reaching even throughout the San'in district.

17 Pray for the newly established YMCA Yonago Medical Welfare Vocational School, that it may offer excellent Christian education. Pray for Christian teachers as they seek to represent the Saviour.

18 Pray that a Christian medical facility may finally be built. Pray for Christian medical workers (physicians, dentists, public health nurses, midwives, nurses, and others).

19 Pray for Christian welfare facilities: Tottori Children's Home for child protection at Tottori City, and Aikokai Home for Mothers and Children at Goko, and for the three church-affiliated preschools.

20 Pray for Christian retreat/camp facilities: YMCA Yobiko Heights Camp. Since there are no Christian book stores in the San'in district, pray that new ways may be found to meet the Christian and non-Christians' need for good literature.

21 Pray for the Christian programs: *True Salvation* and *Lutheran Hour* aired on San'in Radio, and *The Light of The World* on FM San'in. Also, pray for continued healthy fellowship and cooperation among the churches.

Tottori is located on the "back" of Japan, Ura Nihon. *Read Exodus 33:18-23 and ask the Lord in His graciousness to reveal more of His glory to the believers of this prefecture.*

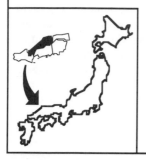

島根 Shimane

Capital: Matsue
Population: 772,601
Cities: 10
  With 1 church: 2
Towns/Villages: 68
  With no churches: 46
  With 20,000 pop. &
  no churches: 1

Size: 6,628 km^2
Density: 117 people/km^2
Churches: P 50, C 4
Church per pop.: 1:15,452
Worship attendance: 894
Attendance/church: 18
Missionaries: 2

Geography

Shimane sits on the Sea of Japan side of the Chugoku mountain ranges. It has a length (northeast - southwest) of 180 kilometers and a width of only 20 - 50 kilometers. Its narrow shape squeezed by the mountain ranges and the shoreline creates many steep hills leaving little room for agriculture. On the east side of the Shimane Peninsula lie the Yasuki and Izumo Plains, the only real farming land in the prefecture. The Oki Islands, four small islands located approximately 40 kilometers away, are part of Shimane. While the eastern region, especially the Izumo area, has heavy rainfalls and occasional hard snowfalls, the Iwami district in the west enjoys relatively warm temperatures and rainy summers.

Industry & Economy

Although Shimane is the 19th largest prefecture, it is one of the least populated. The cultivated land area is very limited with the third lowest agricultural production in the nation. In spite of this, people are very dependent on their agriculture. The fishery industry is declining. This coupled with the suffering mining industry leaves Shimane with only one industry of note, livestock. Beef is a successful business including the prefectural specialty of Shimane Beef. While the average number of cattle per farmer is half that of other prefectures, the total number of cattle is more than double the average, and is the largest in the Chugoku district.

Cultural Background

Izumo was one of the leading cities of ancient times. It was highly advanced even before the Edo era when ocean transportation was the lifeline of culture and industry. Many industries, including steel, were introduced from China via the ocean. Silver mines in Iwami (Omori, present Oda) were directly managed by the Tokugawa administration. At one point their productivity was the highest in Japan. The people are generally conservative. Ishimi residents are more open minded than those of Izumo.

Religious Milieu

The Izumo Shrine has a powerful influence on Shimane's religious climate. Second only to Tottori, the people of Shimane have stronger feelings toward ancestors than any other prefecture. They also have a strong sense of obligation toward family and neighbors, which coupled with traditional beliefs, has hampered people's responsiveness to the more individualistic Christian faith. When they do make a decision, their cultural background can help to develop solid disciples.

The Mission

It appears that during the Edo era there were many silver miners who were secret *Kirishitan* believers. Thirty-six *Kirishitan* exiled from Uragami died as martyrs in Tsuwano. The Catholics returned here in 1868 to reestablish their ministry, and later they were able to build a beautiful church. It became a tourist site over the years, but then was destroyed by arson. Protestant work began with Episcopal missionaries during the early years of Meiji. Their ministry was strengthened by the arrival of B.F. Buxton in 1891. He and other outstanding missionaries of that time have influenced people throughout Japan.

22 Pray for Christian Aishin High School at Gotsu, the only Christian school in the prefecture. Pray that Christian teachers may influence others for Jesus.

23 There seem to be no Christian hospitals or clinics in the prefecture. Pray for Christian workers such as doctors, dentists, public health nurses, midwives, nurses, and others.

24 Other than several church-affiliated preschools, no Christian welfare facilities can be found in the prefecture. Pray that many Christians may rise to the challenge and meet the demands for social services such as nursing homes.

25 There are no Christian retreat centers, camps or book stores in the prefecture. Prayer is needed for more programs which will strengthen and encourage Shimane's Christians. Pray that the Christian programs aired by San'in Radio can be utilized to their fullest in Shimane as well.

26 Pray that the churches in Shimane may develop good fellowship and cooperation. Pray for the Pastors' Associations of Izumo and Ishimi.

Shimane's population has the strongest sense of attachment toward their ancestors among all the prefectures of Japan. Read Matthew 8:21,22 and ask the Lord to turn this deep sense of loyalty and commitment to Christ.

岡山 Okayama

Capital: Okayama City
Population: 1,950,586
Cities: 10
  With 1 church: 2
Towns/Villages: 68
  With no churches: 46
  With 20,000 pop. &
  no churches: 1

Size: 1,868 km^2
Density: 4,600 people/km^2
Churches: P 144, C 10
Church per pop.: 1:13,546
Worship attendance: 4,031
Attendance/church: 28
Missionaries: 15

Geography

Okayama occupies the southeastern region of the Chugoku district. It meets Tottori on the north at the Chugoku district's watershed and Hyogo on the east. The southern part faces the Inland Sea which contains several small islands belonging to Okayama. In the north is the Kibi Highland with a series of small basins, Kuze, Katsuyama and Niimi. From these basins the Yoshii, Asahi and Takahashi Rivers flow southward, creating the wide Okayama Plain in the south. Extending southward into the Inland Sea is the Kojima Peninsula with a bay and lake by the same name. Except for the northern mountainous region, the weather is warm with limited rainfall.

Industry & Economy

With the development of the Mizushima coastal industrial project, Okayama has successfully shifted from agriculture to a manufacturing base. However, Okayama is still a healthy agricultural producer, the best in the Chugoku district, ranking as the top producer of rice, barley, vegetables, and fruits, and nationally it is fourth in grapes and fifth in peaches. The livestock industry is concentrated in the north. The heavy and chemical industries are still growing in the Mizushima area.

Cultural Background

In ancient times the transportation system connecting the two great cultures of Kyushu and Kinki ran through Okayama, exposing the area to both worlds. Since the Edo period Okayama has been well known for its emphasis on education, similar to Nagano's reputation in the east. Partly due to their logical attitude toward life, the people of Okayama bear the reputation of being highly calculative. An awareness survey indicates that more people enjoy work and feel spiritually/mentally fulfilled than in any other prefecture in the nation.

Religious Milieu

The Kibitsu Shrine in Okayama City is a famous religious site, but even more famous are some of the religious leaders this prefecture has produced: Honen (founder of Jodo Buddhism), Eisai (founder of Rinzai Buddhism), and of the newer religions begun at the end of the Edo era, Munetaka Kurozumi (founder of Kurozumikyo) and Bunjiro Kawate (Founder of Konkokyo) to name a few. Kurozumikyo and Konkokyo still have their headquarters in Okayama. Religious interest and the percentage of Shinto believers are higher than the national average. Other noted leaders from this prefecture include Gunpei Yamamuro (founder of the Japan Salvation Army) and Kosuke Tomeoka (founder of Katei School).

The Mission

The *Kirishitan* movement was widespread here. A group of 117 believers, descendants of the *Kirishitan* from Uragami, after being in a kind of confinement by the Okayama government, went back home in 1868. Early Protestant work includes the ministry of Tsurin Kanemori and the founding of an orphanage by Juji Ishii. After the War church planting took place throughout the prefecture, and a long lasting fellowship of Christian leaders called *Senkyo no Tsudoi* has been a good support to the Evangelical work in the whole area.

27 Pray for Sanyo Gakuen and Junsei Jr College. Both began as Christian schools. Pray for the Tsuyama Social Education and Culture Foundation, founded 70 years ago, as they administer the Tsuyama Christian Library, Tsuyama Science Education and Folklore Museums.

28 Pray for the Okayama Hakuaikai Hospital which has been serving the community for over 100 years, and for its affiliated nursing home, Adams Home. Pray for preschools run by churches or individual Christians.

29 Pray for Hiruzen Bible Camp at Yatsuka and the Youth Center at Ushimado. Pray for the CLC Christian book store at Okayama.

30 Pray for the Christian ministry of the *Voice of Hope* and the *Lutheran Hour* aired on Sanyo Radio. Unfortunately no TV programs are available.

31 Pray for the Okayama *Senkyo no Tsudoi* as it pulls together the various churches. Also pray for the Okayama City Christian Teachers Association, North Okayama Pastors' Fellowship, Kurashiki City Pastors' Fellowship, and the Bizen District Pastors' Fellowship.

Okayama's people seem to have a deeper sense of spiritual/emotional fulfillment than any other prefecture. Read Ecclesiastes 3:11 and ask the Lord to disturb this false sense of fulfillment and cause the people of Okayama to become "restless until they find their rest in Him."

広島 Hiroshima

Capital: Hiroshima City
Population: 2,870,671
Cities: 13
  With 1 church: 0
Towns/Villages: 73
  With no churches: 59
  With 20,000 pop. &
  no churches: 2

Size: 8,467 km²
Density: 339 people/km²
Churches: P 167, C 14
Church per pop.: 1:17,190
Worship attendance: 4,670
Attendance/church: 28
Missionaries: 15

Geography

Hiroshima is located in the central area of the Chugoku district. Its south faces the Inland Sea, the east borders Okayama, the northeast Tottori, to the north is Shimane, and the west is Yamaguchi. The Chugoku mountain chain, stretching from north to northwest along the border eventually merges with the Kamuriyama mountains at the west border. The eastern region has the Miyoshi Basin and the Kibi Plain; near the sea is the Fukuyama Plain. In the west is the Hiroshima Plain, extending all the way to Hiroshima Bay. In the Inland Sea are approximately 150 islands belonging to Hiroshima, of which 40 are inhabited.

Industry & Economy

Hiroshima has both the most land and the largest population in the Chugoku and Shikoku districts, ranking 11th and 12th in the nation, respectively. In total agricultural production it also ranks high. The leading industry is commerce and manufacturing, with automobile, steel and clothing industries ranked fifth nationally. The areas around Fukuyama, Onomichi, Hiroshima/Kure are key industrial development regions. In the fishing industry, over 60% of Japan's oysters comes from Hiroshima.

Cultural Background

From the Meiji era to the end of World War II, the city of Hiroshima prospered as the center of the military industry. Kure was a naval port, while the adjacent city of Edajima was the headquarters of the naval academy. The great devastation caused by the atomic bombing pushed Hiroshima to become a force for world peace with its motto, "No More Hiroshima." Accelerated reconstruction efforts led to a healthy economic recovery by the city, but small farming and mountain villages, as well as the Inland Sea islands have been left behind in their development.

Religious Milieu

The famous Itsukushima Shrine, praised as one of the three most beautiful views in Japan, is now more popular as a tourist site than as a place of worship. Hiroshima has the highest percentage of Buddhist believers in the Chugoku district. The popular Jodo Shinshu Buddhism plays an important role in providing spiritual support for Hiroshima, not just as a traditional community organizational system as is so common in other parts of Japan. This powerful tie has caused resistance to the gospel since the Meiji era.

The Mission

There is a significantly lower number of churches per population in the rural communities than in the city. Many small, hard-to-reach mountain communities are unchurched. Church planters in cities like Hiroshima struggle to keep up with the population increase. An aggressive church planting ministry is especially needed in these high population areas, which will then reach out into the mountain communities.

1 Pray for the Christian schools; Hiroshima Women's School (jr high, high school and college), Hiroshima YMCA Gakuen: Business School, Social Work School, Design and Drafting School, and Fukuyama YMCA International Business School.

2 Pray for the Christian medical facility, Kawamura Hospital in Hiroshima, and for the Christian welfare facilities: Salvation Army Aiko Home for children at Kure, Tsuda Home for Children at Saeki; for The Kure Jiai Ryo for women, and Hiroshima Seiko Gakuen at Mihara and Seikei Jusanjo at Takehara, both of which minister to the physically disabled.

3 Pray for the Christian retreat/camp facilities: Hiroshima YMCA Minochi Lodge at Yuki and the YMCA Hall equipped to also handle wedding ceremonies. Pray for the Christian book stores: CLC Books and Seibun Book Store, both at Hiroshima City.

4 Pray that the prefecture may have a televised ministry program and that from there it may expand to the rest of Sanyo. Pray for *Light of The World*, *Voice of Hope*, and *True Salvation* aired on Chugoku Radio.

5 Pray that churches may be started in the mountain villages and the small islands of the Inland Sea. Also, pray for good fellowship and cooperation among the pastors in the prefecture.

Hiroshima was the first place to experience the effects of atomic weapons. Many emotional scars remain. This has given rise to many peace movements coming from the city of Hiroshima. Read Isaiah 9:6 and ask the Lord to reveal the glory of His risen Christ to the people of the prefecture.

September 6~10

山口 Yamaguchi

Capital: Yamaguchi City
Population: 1,550,419
Cities: 14
  With 1 church: 2
Towns/Villages: 42
  With no churches: 31
  With 20,000 pop. &
   no churches: 0

Size: 6,106 km^2
Density: 254 people/km^2
Churches: P 97, C 16
Church per pop.: 1:15,984
Worship attendance: 2,047
Attendance/church: 21
Missionaries: 29

Geography

This westernmost prefecture of Honshu Island, Yamaguchi, is sandwiched between the Sea of Japan and the Inland Sea. Yamaguchi also shares an eastern border with Shimane and Hiroshima. The 700-meter-wide Kammon Channel separates Yamaguchi and Kyushu Island along with islands such as Yashiro Island (Oshima). The Chugoku mountain range changes as it approaches western Yamaguchi, from imposing mountains to mild highlands of no more than 500 meters. The climate is typical of that around the Sea of Japan. Yamaguchi is susceptible to damage caused by wind and rain storms.

Industry & Economy

The prefectural agricultural production is about average for both the region and the nation. Compared to the other industries, agriculture/forestry does not play a critical role. However, rice, barley, citrus fruits, and lotus roots are prefectural specialties. Yamaguchi is blessed with good fishing ports such as Shimonoseki, excellent shore fishing, and is still considered one of the top producers of shrimp and sea bream. However, the fishing industry has been declining. The cement and heavy chemicals are growing industries.

Cultural Background

In ancient times Yamaguchi was part of the Kyushu cultural district, receiving considerable influence from China. This gave the prefecture a fairly high level of culture. Even after the power shifted eastward, it maintained good relationships with the Yamato government. Since the Sengoku Civil War era, the Mori family, the power of Yamaguchi, controlled the entire Chugoku district from Yamaguchi. After the Meiji Restoration, many members of the family were assigned to posts in the Meiji administration. In fact, Yamaguchi has produced several prime-ministers.

Religious Milieu

A recent survey showed that 70% of Yamaguchi believes that the emperor should be given the utmost respect. This is the highest in the nation. An equal percent believe that the old customs and traditions should be valued. This ranked fourth nationally. And yet they only show an average interest in religion, and have no specially famous temple or shrine. They were second highest in the nation for feeling that it is important to obey the national and local governments. These attitudes, coupled with their strong group feelings, make it difficult for them to make individual decisions for the gospel.

The Mission

Christian work in Yamaguchi was begun by St. Francis Xavier himself. He was given an open door by Lord Ouchi, which led to many conversions. The Protestant ministry began in Shimonoseki. Knowing the success of the prewar missionary activities in the midst of an inflexible and conservative environment should spur us on to reach this prefecture.

6 Pray for the Christian schools: Baiko Women's Gakuin (jr high and high schools, jr college, and college) at Shimonoseki, which has been offering Christian education for over 100 years. Also remember Seiko High School at Hikari with 70 years of history.

7 There are no Christian medical clinics and hospitals. Pray that the Christian medical workers will be able to share Christ's love in the midst of their work.

8 Pray for the Kame no Ie ministry at Shuto, an apartment for severely disabled, training them to lead independent lives. There are only two church-affiliated preschools in Yamaguchi, but each year they are teaching many children about the Living God.

9 There are no Christian book stores and training centers. Pray that Christians be encouraged to grow and become stronger. Pray for *The Light of The World* and *Children of the Star* aired on Yamaguchi Radio, and also for *Hit Pop Request* aired on FM Yamaguchi.

10 Pray for healthy fellowship and cooperation among pastors and churches. Pray for interdenominational groups: The *Light of The World* Sponsor Fellowship, two branches of the Gideon Association, the Morning Prayer Meetings at Ube and Shimonoseki, and others.

Yamaguchi, as a prefecture, has one of the strongest "group mentalities" in Japan. Read Acts 11:13-14; 16:31-32, ask the Lord to use this strong group/family mentality, that has been a tool to resist the gospel, to bring redemption to the families and social structures of this prefecture.

 # 四国 Shikoku District

Population: 4,220,707	Size: 18,806 km²
Cities: 30	Density: 224 people/km²
With no churches: 0	Churches: P 328, C 34
With 1 church: 3	Church per pop.: 1:12,868
Towns/Villages: 186	Worship attendance: 8,283
With no churches: 114	Attendance/church: 25
With 20,000 pop. &	Attendance/pop.: 0.20
no churches: 1	Missionaries: 21

Compared with the other districts in Japan, Shikoku has a relatively high number of churches, 328 in all. In fact, all four prefectures in this district have a higher ratio than the national average. Kagawa is second only to Okinawa for the largest number of churches per population in the nation. However, the district growth in number of churches started in the last ten years is the worst in the nation, with only 37 churches added in the past 10 years. 16 of these were started in Kagawa. A number of these new churches were the result of efforts by Ralph Cox (TEAM) and his cooperating missionaries. He has been able to begin these churches and then successfully turn them over to Japanese pastors. During the Meiji era, the missionaries from the Southern Presbyterian Church (USA) ventured into the remote mountain villages to share the gospel. Many leaders of small villages became Christians and the ministries grew. The ridge-end tiles engraved with a cross on the old tombstones still stand as a powerful witness to their faith.

11 Pray for many pilgrims who come to Mt. Tsurugi and Mt. Ishizuchi to worship the god, Kompira. What they seek can be found in Christ. We Christians can gladly follow Him, making at least the level of sacrifice these pilgrims make. Pray a special blessing of encouragement on the 17,000 Christians in the Shikoku district!

12 Pray that the 114 unchurched villages and towns hear the Word and that believers join in church fellowships. One of these is the town of Kagawa in Kagawa prefecture with a population of 24,000. There are three cities which have only one Protestant church: Iyo-Mishima in Ehime, Tosa and Muroto in Kochi. Pray that through the Shikoku All-Christian Retreat Christians will become Spirit controlled and active witnesses.

An Aging Japan

There is an increasing number of elderly people in our modern society. In 1980, 9% of the population was 65 years and older. In 1990, the number increased to 12%, and in 1995 to 15%. Aging is a social problem that affects every aspect of our country from the nation's economy to our Christian ministries. When Christians become older, they are not able to attend worship services. Some will not be able to take care of themselves and will be institutionalized in nursing homes or cared for by their families. Churches will need to share in this responsibility.

The growing number of older people is also reflected in the pastors. A large percentage of present pastors will need to retire in several years, greatly decreasing the available number of pastors. There are not enough younger pastors to fill these vacant spots. Now is the time to educate and train a younger generation so that these vacancies can be filled. Another possible answer for this shortage is the trained lay leader. Perhaps this will be a great opportunity for the layperson.

With the increasing number of elderly people we will also have greater opportunity to share the gospel and welcome older seekers into our fellowship. As people approach the aging phase of their lives, they often seek spiritual peace. Thus, the ministry of Christian nursing homes and hospice services will take on new potential.

13 Every person, male or female, is equal in the eyes of God. The gospel does not support discrimination. However, within Christian churches and especially in this sinful world, women have been greatly discriminated against. Pray that they be treated as equal partners in society and in church.

14 The discrimination against the disabled is another problem of our society. Christianity has for years taken the lead in ministering to them. Pray that throughout our society they may be accepted with equal rights.

15 Pray for the Japan King's Garden Association. It was founded in 1980 with the blessing of the Japan Evangelical Association (JEA). There are now nursing home facilities at Tsukuba, Kawagoe, Mie, Tokyo, Miyagi, Sendai, Kanazawa and other places.

16 Pray for the Evangelical Medical Fellowship (EMF). It serves as a support group for Evangelical Christians in the medical field. Its work includes coordinating seminars and overseas training trips. These programs are a part of their goal to strengthen the members' faith and build sound fellowship among them so that each member is able to accomplish his/her mission as a Christian.

徳島 Tokushima

Capital: Tokushima City
Population: 837,570
Cities: 4
  With 1 church: 0
Towns/Villages: 46
  With no churches: 31
  With 20,000 pop. &
    no churches: 0

Size: 4,145 km^2
Density: 202 people/km^2
Churches: P 55, C 4
Church per pop.: 1:15,229
Worship attendance: 1,478
Attendance/church: 27
Missionaries: 1

Geography

Tokushima occupies the eastern section of Shikoku Island. Tall mountain ranges, 1,000 - 2,000 meters high, hedge its north and west sides. The east and southeast face the Pacific Ocean and the Kii Channel. In the north, the Yoshino River runs parallel to the Sanuki Mountain Range, forming the Tokushima Plain, the only plain in the prefecture, before flowing into the ocean. The Tsurugi Mountains in the center and south extend to the ocean bluffs. There is little rain in the north, while the south experiences the rough Pacific Ocean climate that includes heavy rainfall and typhoons.

Industry & Economy

Tokushima depends on agriculture, forestry and fisheries. The percentage of agricultural workers and productivity is the second largest in Shikoku next to Kochi. Rice fields occupy the lower region of the Yoshino River and the small, narrow plains along the shore. Much of the remaining land is used for vegetables and flowers. The prefecture is the nation's largest supplier of cauliflower and lotus roots, and the fourth largest producer of carrots. Japanese indigo is only produced here. Industrial development is taking place around the Tokushima and Naruto districts. This growth should accelerate once Shikoku gains easy access to the Hanshin Industrial district through the Akashi Channel's new bridge connecting Shikoku and Honshu.

Cultural Background

Since the Edo era, Tokushima has had a thriving commerce, giving the people an image of being highly competitive and money-oriented. Women in the work place have made a major economic contribution, and Tokushima has more female company presidents than any other prefecture in the nation. The Awa Odori Festival (carnival), held every August, has gained national and worldwide attention. Perhaps it is a way for the people to express their resistance to Japan's conservatism.

Religious Milieu

The people of Tokushima value family name and status more than any other prefecture, and feel very spiritually connected to their ancestors (tenth highest in nation and first in Shikoku). Although Tokushima's Ryusen Temple in Naruto is the first stop on an 88-temple pilgrimage of the Shikoku district, there are not many traditional Buddhist followers here. This is due in part to the influence of Soka Gakkai and sectarian Shintoism, with their emphasis on material blessings. Response to the gospel is also often tied to the possibility of gain or loss.

The Mission

Although he later abandoned his faith, when Lord Suka Hachi became a *Kirishitan,* many others followed him. In the early years of the Meiji era, 116 so called Uragami Christians were exiled here. The Protestant work began with Episcopal missionaries, followed by the Southern Presbyterian Church from the United States. One fruit of the work was Toyohiko Kagawa who became an outstanding Christian leader and social reformer. The inspiring postwar ministry of Eiichi Ito led to the founding of churches in farming communities like Kamojima, Wakimachi, and Sadamitsu.

17 Tokushima is the only prefecture in Shikoku that has no Christian schools. Pray that Christian teachers provide a good example to young people and have a positive influence on their life.

18 Pray for the Christian hospitals: Tokushima Eiko and Oshima at Wakimachi. Also pray for health-related workers such as doctors, dentists, public health nurses, midwives, nurses, and others.

19 Pray for the Kamo Charity House, ministering to the physically weak. Pray for many church-affiliated or Christian managed preschools.

20 Pray for Osaka YMCA Anan International Marine Center and Tokushima Christian Center Book Store. Pray that Christian TV programs become available, and for *The Light of the World, Children of Star, Voice of Hope,* and *Lutheran Hour,* all aired on Shikoku Radio.

21 Pray for good fellowship and cooperation among churches through the Tokushima Ministers Fellowship, Shikoku Radio Ministry Fellowship, and the Tokushima Area Christmas Evangelistic Outreach. Pray for churches to be established in the many unchurched villages and towns.

Tokushima's people are known for valuing their family name more highly than anywhere else in Japan. Read Philippians 2:9,10 and ask the Lord to bring a new loyalty to the "name that is above every other name" for the families of this prefecture.

Ancestor Worship
The Great Hindrance to the Gospel

Japan's population is approximately 125 million, but the total number of religious adherents is 220 million. These are roughly divided into the following:

Shinto	110,000,000
Buddhist	100,000,000
Christian	1,500,000
Other	11,000,000

However, 9,000,000 are actually registered at a Shinto shrine, and the rest of the number comes from all those who are related to local guardian gods. As for Buddhism, most of the numbers come from families related to local temples with no consideration for individual faith. The "Other" category is hard to analyze, but the Christian statistics are based on solid confessions of faith. The fact that many people are counted in several categories is not strange to the Japanese. The celebration of a baby's birth takes place at the Shinto shrine; the wedding ceremony might be Christian or Shinto, and Buddhist priests will be in charge of the funeral. This mixture is just part of the Japanese life style.

In speaking of the Shinto shrine system, we must remember that the shrines were forcefully separated from the Buddhist temples at the beginning of the Meiji era. Previously they had been intertwined for a long period of time. Buddhism came to Japan from India through China, and has been considerably modified. The unique indigenous belief of Japan became mixed with Buddhism which had already been modified by the Confucianism of China.

Ancestor worship, which is not part of the Indian belief of reincarnation, along with the practices centered around the equinox and *Obon,* were either part of ancient Japan, or they were brought here from China and Korea.

The Japanese people, their language, culture and religion, whether Shinto, Buddhist or the newer religions, all join together in ancestor worship. How to respond to the problem of ancestor worship is a key issue for evangelism. Evangelical Christians stand on the Word of God which prohibits the worshipping of ancestors. And yet we are also bound to show honor and respect.

22 The religions of Japan have ancestor worship as their common denominator. The Bible does not prohibit honoring ancestors, but says that it is a sin to worship them as gods. Pray that many Japanese be delivered from their belief in ancestor worship.

23 Pray for churches that need cemetery plots so that they can provide an alternative Christian burial. Pray for wisdom for Christians as they attend non-Christian funerals that they may show love and respect, while maintaining a Christian witness.

24 In the midst of the uncountable number of religions, pray that many Japanese will see their error and come to know life in Christ.

25 Many cults that seek to pass themselves off as Christian are rapidly spreading. Especially pray for those people involved with Jehovah's Witnesses that they will understand the truth in Christ.

26 Pray for those involved in groups like the Moonies whose activities include socially unacceptable and even illegal actions.

27 Many churches are busy planning their fall evangelistic meetings. Pray that God would richly bless the preparations and that many would make salvation decisions.

28 Pray for Christian young people as they prepare for marriage. Pray that they would choose the right person, and that their wedding and married life would be based on God's love and blessing.

29 Over half of the non-Christian young people in Japan desire to have a Christian Western-style wedding. This has become a great opportunity for evangelistic witness. Pray that the Lord would guide those Christian leaders and organizations like the Christian Bridal Mission and the Japan Bridal Missions Association.

The Jehovah's Witnesses now have 213,000 baptized believers with an additional 236,000 seekers in their study program. Last year they spent 100 million hours in evangelism. The growth is so phenomenal that the average Japanese is beginning to think of normal Christianity as Jehovah's Witness religion. There are several groups that are specifically seeking to reach these people: Word of Truth Ministries led by William Wood and Ministry for the Salvation of the Jehovah's Witnesses with Pastor Sadao Kusakari are both active in seminars, publishing and counselling; Jehovah's Witnesses To Christ (JWTC) led by Pastor Keisuke Nakazawa is very active in research, publishing and seminars.

香川 Kagawa

Capital: Takamatsu
Population: 1,033,671
Cities: 5
 With 1 church: 0
Towns/Villages: 38
 With no churches: 18
 With 20,000 pop. &
 no churches: 1

Size: 1,882 km^2
Density: 549 people/km^2
Churches: P 88, C 14
Church per pop.: 1:11,746
Worship attendance: 1,963
Attendance/church: 22
Missionaries: 10

Geography

Kagawa occupies the northeastern region of Shikoku and stretches east and west as a long narrow neck. The northern area of Kagawa faces the Inland Sea and includes numerous islands of varying sizes, such as Shodo Island. The Sanuki Plain is in the center with the Sanuki Mountain Chain in the south. Tokushima is on the south, while the western border slightly touches Ehime prefecture. Kagawa has the nation's smallest total area. The climate is typical of the Inland Sea with little rainfall and warm temperatures all year round. Over 20,000 irrigation ponds have been created to offset this shortage of rainfall.

Industry & Economy

Unlike other prefectures in the Shikoku district, the agriculture industry does not contribute much to Kagawa's economy. However, many patches of flat lands, including highland areas, enable double-cropping, which increases agriculture's contribution. The most successful products are lettuce (3rd in the nation) and onions (highest in the Shikoku district). Aquaculture, a more controlled way of farming the ocean, is much more successful than the fishing industry, ranking as the largest producer of yellowtail tuna and the second largest producer of seaweed in the Shikoku and Chugoku districts. The industrial district is centered along the coastline between Takamatsu and Kannonji, where future growth is expected upon completion of the Seto Bridge.

Cultural Background

Because of its closeness to Honshu Island, Kagawa has been a gateway to Shikoku Island. New cultures and merchandise were brought by the settlers and visitors to the Kotohiragu Shrine, making Kagawa the gateway to the rest of the Island. The people are conservative and are said to lack a cooperative spirit. The mild climate and lack of natural disasters are credited for the people's tendencies to be mellow, modest, hard-working, optimistic, and fun-loving in leisure.

Religious Milieu

The people of Kagawa show an interest in religion, especially in Buddhism. The percentage of Buddhists is the highest in both Chugoku and Shikoku. The popularity of Buddhism can be directly related to the prefecture's history: Kobo Daishi (the Great Teacher Kobo) was born here. Also, out of 88 temples on the Shikoku pilgrimage route, 22 temples (from 67th to 88th) exist here. A clear example of the mixing of Buddhism and Shintoism is seen in the Kotohiragu Shrine, where Kompira, a god whose origin comes from Indian Buddhism, is regarded as the guardian deity of seafarers. Because of this religious climate, Kagawa is rather behind in pursuing an individualistic faith.

The Mission

It seems that the spread of Christianity was limited in Kagawa's past. The ministry in Kagawa was begun by foreign missionaries in the early years of the Meiji era. In 1899 the Baptist church launched a unique boat ministry traveling throughout the islands spreading Christianity from their boat, *Fukuin* (Gospel). In the postwar era, a ministry headed by Ralph Cox, TEAM missionary, has led to the founding of many churches. The missionaries of the Southern Presbyterian Church founded the Shikoku Gakuin University. The churches and the university are strengthening the presence of Christianity in these communities.

30 Pray for Shikoku Gakuin University (jr college and university at Zentsuji). Also pray that Christian jr high and high schools can be started.

1 Pray for the Christian ministry of Eikokai Luke Hospital in Takamatsu and for the Christian social facilities for the elderly: Zion's Hill Home at Takamatsu, Makino Village Airo Home, and Kozanso at Iiyama.

2 Pray for Kobe YMCA Yoshima Outdoor Activity Center, the Christian training center. Pray for Life Center book store at Takamatsu and for their work in helping Christians grow.

3 Pray for the Christian television ministry: *Harvest Time* on West Japan Broadcast. Remember the Christian radio ministries: *Lutheran Hour*, *Bible and You*, and *Career Midnight Cruise*, aired on FM Kagawa.

4 Pray that pastors and churches have good cooperation and fellowship and for the assisting services of the Takamatsu Ministers' Conference, the Takamatsu Missionary Prayer Meeting, the Kagawa Evangelical Pastors' Meeting, and the Kagawa Mission Liaison Committee.

Kagawa is known for its limited rainfall and water resources. Read Isaiah 41:18-20 and ask the Lord to create new, "living water" resources within the church for the people of Kagawa.

愛媛 Ehime

Capital: Matsuyama
Population: 1,523,471
Cities: 12
 With 1 church: 1
Towns/Villages: 58
 With no churches: 33
 With 20,000 pop. &
  no churches: 0

Size: 5,672 km^2
Density: 269 people/km^2
Churches: P 125, C 11
Church per pop.: 1:12,188
Worship attendance: 3,247
Attendance/church: 26
Missionaries: 6

Geography

Ehime occupies the northwest region of Shikoku, facing the Inland Sea on the north and the Bungo Channel on the west. On the northeast are Kagawa and Tokushima prefectures, while its southeastern boundary touches Kochi at the Shikoku Mountain Chain. Its slender shape stretches 150 kilometers from northeast to southwest. Along the Inland Sea coastline, there are three major plains: Niihama, Imabari and Matsuyama. The Takanawa Peninsula lies between the Imabari and Matsuyama Plains. The Sata Cape is the tip of the Ishizuchi Mountain Chain, located in the west. The climate of the north is typical of the Inland Sea, while the south experiences the Pacific Ocean weather with heavy rainfall. Mt. Ishizuchi, Shikoku's highest peak, remains snow-capped till the end of April.

Industry & Economy

Although the agricultural industry is declining, Ehime still has more cultivated land and its gross product is higher than that of any other prefecture in Shikoku. The production of *mikan* (tangerines), ranks number one, supplying over 75% of the national production, and total fruit is the highest of the western prefectures. The fishery industry is healthy, with the highest haul in all of Shikoku. The ocean farming industry is also quite successful, accounting for 1/3 of the marine industry in the prefecture. Ehime is also a top producer of cultured sea bream and is the second highest producer of yellowtail tuna. The manufacturing industry has developed around the Niihama and Toyo districts.

Cultural Background

Ehime is filled with ancient history. An example of this is that the Dogo Hot Spring in Matsuyama is mentioned in the Manyoshu, a collection of ancient poems known to be the oldest in the country. The climate is consistently mild and natural disasters are few. As a result the people of Ehime are said to be mild natured as symbolized by the name, Ehime, meaning "maiden." They are submissive to authority and tradition, emphatic on community issues, and yet very shy towards strangers.

Religious Milieu

Since many Ehime temples are included in the Shikoku Pilgrimage, there is no lack of interest in religion. However, it is rather surprising to find them open to other religions, since they are known to emphasize tradition and submission to authority. Ehime has one of the highest percentages of church attendance in all of Kinki, Chugoku, and Shikoku districts. Protestant missionaries first came to Shikoku in the early Meiji era, and the island's first church was started in Imabari in 1878. A mission school and churches from various denominations were established early in Matsuyama.

The Mission

The fact that the very first Protestant church in Shikoku was established here, along with certain historical and sociological influences should give us hope for the future of the church here. Matsuyama has hosted the All-Shikoku Christian Retreat and leaders from there still provide the impetus for its continuation. While Ehime, as a whole, is experiencing a population decrease, seven out of the 12 cities in the prefecture are growing. This population trend should influence future evangelistic planning.

5 Pray for these schools with a long Christian background: Matsuyama Shinonome Gakuen (jr high and high school, women's jr college, women's college) and Matsuyama Gakuin (Matsuyama Jonan High School). Also pray for Ayumi Gakuen in Matsuyama, and their ministry to the disabled.

6 Pray for Matsuyama Bethel Hospital, for Matsuyama Garden of Eden and Bethel Home, both for the elderly, and Galilee Home at Kawauchi for the elderly with special care needs.

7 Pray for the Christian retreat centers: Usagino Yama Izumi no Ie Camp (A Holiness facility at Saijo) and Matsuyama Seibi Kaikan. Pray for the Christian book stores: Christian Book Store and Ark Book Store, both at Matsuyama.

8 Pray that evangelistic TV programs will be broadcast in the near future. Pray for *The Light of The World* and *True Salvation* aired on Nankai Radio. Especially pray that these ministries will touch people in areas where there are no churches.

9 Pray for good fellowship and cooperation between churches and pastors. Pray that Ehime, as an organizer of the All-Shikoku Christian Retreat which started in Ehime, continues to be a blessing to the whole island.

Ehime means "maiden," an unmarried young woman. Read Revelation 21:2, 9-11 and ask the Lord to encourage the Christians (Church) in this prefecture, as the bride of Christ, that they have a Husband. May they understand and be renewed by the knowledge of their relationship with Christ.

Men in the Workplace

It is not just in the Japanese church that women's groups are so strong. It is true in other countries and other religions as well. In the past the Japanese church had a disproportionate number of young people. Now, it is the women, and as the Japan society ages, most likely the elderly will become the majority. But it always has been true that the least represented group is the working-aged man, especially the fathers. The Japanese father also tends to be missing from the home. Even though his influence should be indispensable, his presence is not felt. The same is true in the church.

Even though a Christian may be very concerned about his faith, he most likely is very diligent at his work, which in turn makes church attendance a growing burden. Also, it is very difficult for him to lead his fellow-workers to Jesus. It is crucial for churches to pray for and seek to develop effective ways to reach men. We have learned that to reach students we need to target the schools. Most of the men's time is spent at work, and similarly we need to penetrate the working place. In the Western world there are many examples of special fellowship and evangelistic groups developed by medical, military, postal workers, etc. to reach their fellow workers. Perhaps it is easier for this kind of work to evolve where there are unions and more of a horizontal based society. This is difficult in Japan with its strong vertical society.

It is difficult to get busy businessmen together, but we need to be more creative in thinking of new ways. Company leaders can gather for a breakfast meeting. After work hours is very difficult because of the long hours and the uncertainty of their schedules. Around Japan a number of Christian groups are beginning to use the breakfast hour as a time for fellowship and evangelism. We must work hard to reach the men and fathers of Japan.

10 Sports Day

Pray for the salvation of athletes and sports leaders. The Japanese youth especially look up to these stars. Pray for the few Christian athletes that they have an effective testimony. Foreign Christian baseball, basketball and soccer players at times play in the professional leagues here. Friendship Golf is an example of groups seeking to reach the athletes.

11 Pray for the witness of the few Christians who are involved in the entertainment world of theater, cinema, etc. Pray that the Lord would raise up a strong movement among these people.

12 Evangelicals have banded together to form an interdenominational fellowship called the Japan Christian Laypeople's Conference. The purpose is for fellowship and evangelism. Stand with them in prayer.

13 Pray for the ministry and fellowship of the Japan Christian Business Men's Conference (CBMC). There are now seven active groups in Japan.

14 This is Railroad Founding Day in Japan. Pray for Christian railroad workers who have Railroad Gospel Fellowships in each of the Japan railroad companies. Especially remember the Christians who are seeking to witness to their peers.

15 Pray for the Christian Business Men's Association (CBA). The purpose of the group is to encourage Christians to be faithful to the Bible and to live righteous and dynamic lives in the workplace.

16 Pray for the Japan International Gideon Society. As in other parts of the world, they are active in Bible distribution at schools, hotels, prisons, etc. Most Japanese receive their first New Testament from a Gideon.

17 The *Chotokai*, (Morning Prayer Group) was started by a business man in Osaka and has now spread throughout Japan. Pray that this movement will continue to grow, maintaining healthy fellowship and spiritual power in prayer.

高知 Kochi

Capital: Kochi City
Population: 825,995
Cities: 9
　With 1 church: 2
　Towns/Villages: 44
　With no churches: 32
　With 20,000 pop. &
　no churches: 0

Size: 7,107 km^2
Density: 116 people/km^2
Churches: P 60, C 5
Church per pop.: 1:13,767
Worship attendance: 1,595
Attendance/church: 27
Missionaries: 4

Geography

Kochi, the largest prefecture in the Shikoku district, occupies the southern half of Shikoku Island and faces the Pacific Ocean on the south. It shares a prefectural line with Tokushima and Ehime on the north. Kochi is 180 kilometers long, and layers of mountains take up most of its land leaving only two plains, Kochi and Nakamura. It is the least populated prefecture in Shikoku and has the fourth lowest population density in the nation. Tosa Bay, famous for its mouth measuring 130 kilometers across, holds Muroto Cape on the east, and Ashizuri Cape on the west. Kochi has warm temperatures and heavy rainfalls with hot and humid summers. It enjoys an average of only 70 sunny days a year, and also receives considerable damage from seasonal typhoons.

Industry & Economy

Even though only Miyagi prefecture has a higher percentage of farmers, Kochi's agricultural gross product is not impressive because of lack of cultivated land. Rice production is not enough to supply its own demand, and fruit production is also inadequate. Egg plant production is the highest in the nation and bell peppers are third. Forests take up 80% of the land, providing a thriving forestry industry. The fishing industry is also healthy. Although the total haul might not be high, bonito (second only to Shizuoka's catch) and tuna are outstanding.

Cultural Background

Compared to the three other Shikoku prefectures, Kochi possesses a slightly different culture due to the geographical separation from the rest of the area by the number of mountains. The main cultural influence since the medieval era is believed to have been directly from Kyoto via ocean traffic. The people are known to be extremely stubborn, anti-authority prone, and have less respect for the government, the emperor and elders than the average.

Religious Milieu

A study shows that the people of Kochi are rather indifferent to religion and faith. As a result, the pilgrimage temples (24th to 39th) of this prefecture do not create as much attention as the other prefectures in this district. History states that 126 Uragami Christians exiled to Kochi from Nagasaki in 1868 (Meiji 1) were able to pursue their faith thanks to the kindness shown to them by the people. Even though there is a low level of interest in religion here, it is surprising that following Wakayama and Nara, Kochi has the third highest number of Shinto believers. The influence of tradition and lack of religious interest has limited people's interest in other faiths.

The Mission

Foreign missionaries first introduced Protestant Christianity here and were able to prepare for later church planting ministries. The Southern Presbyterian missionaries from the USA, especially the McIlwain father-son team, are worthy of note. They were able to reach into even some of the most remote mountain areas.

18 Pray for Seiwa Gakuen (girls' jr high and high schools in Kochi), which is about to celebrate a century of ministry. Pray that they hold to a Christian based education. Pray that Christians teaching in secular schools give a clear testimony for Christ.

19 There seems to be no Christian medical facility or social service available. Pray for the Christians who are involved in secular medical and social work.

20 Pray for the ministry of the Kochi Gospel Book Store. It is difficult to carry on the book ministry with a low population base and small number of Christians.

21 Pray that the radio ministry reaches mountain villages and small communities that have no churches. The two radio broadcasts are *Invitation Hour to Christianity* and *True Salvation* aired by Kochi Radio.

22 Pray for good fellowship and cooperation between pastors and churches. Pray for the Kochi Evangelical Fellowship, and that the Shikoku Revival Prayer Fellowship be a blessing.

Kochi's introduction to the gospel was spearheaded by a missionary father and son team. Read Acts 13:2 and ask the Lord to birth such zeal and team work for church planting among the Japanese men of the church.

Denominations and Church Associations

Some people think that there are too many Christian denominations. However, in contrast to Buddhism where each sect has its own scriptures, Christian groups are united around the same Bible. In addition to the Bible, Catholicism states that the Church carries equal authority with the Bible. Within the Protestant churches various groups were formed at the time of the Reformation because of regional differences, teachings concerning certain biblical truths, and particular charismatic leaders.

The more well-known Protestant groups include Lutheran, Reform/Presbyterian (Calvin), Mennonite, and Baptist. The Anglican Church (Episcopal in Japan) began in England during the Reformation. An attempt to reform the Anglican Church resulted in the birth of Methodism, which later gave birth to the Holiness movement. Pentecostals have placed strong emphasis on the Holy Spirit and His gifts. This emphasis has had a broad impact on many different groups.

23 Pray for leaders of different denominations and fellowships. We should not let denominational issues slow our ministry down. Pray that leaders will be spiritually mature, not ministering from a sense of competition. May the many denominations in Japan be a great blessing.

24 Pray for leaders of the different para-church groups. Remember those groups that are especially struggling to accomplish God's will with limited finances. Pray that God will raise up those who will financially support these groups, and that new workers will feel led to minister with these groups.

25 Pray for Christians who have become separated from their churches. Often they suffer from doubts and temptations and become targets for other religious groups. Pray that they will be led back into fellowship. Pray churches and pastors will have God's wisdom in how to help them.

26 This fall many evangelistic meetings are taking place. Pray that the seekers attending the churches will make salvation decisions, and also that many new people will attend these meetings and become regulars.

October 27~28

九州、沖縄 **Kyushu, Okinawa**

Population: 14,707,601
Cities: 93
  With no churches: 2
  With 1 church: 20
Towns/Villages: 477
  With no churches: 358
  With 20,000 pop. &
  no churches: 11

Size: 43,678 km²
Density: 337 people/km²
Churches: P 861, C 317
Church per pop.: 1:17,082
Worship attendance: 27,241
Attendance/church: 32
Attendance/pop.: 0.71
Missionaries: 239

Christianity has its longest and deepest roots in the Kyushu district. Francis Xavier and the Jesuits arrived in Kagoshima in 1549. Christianity spread to Okinawa, Tane Island, and Kagoshima, and then to other areas of Kyushu and Japan until it was made illegal and severely oppressed. Many died as martyrs and many others abandoned their faith. Some sought to keep their faith as secret *Kirishitan*, and Christianity vanished from the public eye.

When Catholic missionaries resumed their work in the Meiji era, they were amazed to find secret *Kirishitan* who had survived the persecution. Because of the long years of isolation their faith had become very corrupted, to the extent that it often was difficult for the *Kirishitan* and the missionaries to clearly identify each other as having the same faith. Protestant missionaries also came to Kyushu at the beginning of Meiji with work centering around Nagasaki, Kumamoto, and Saga. The work of the Southern Baptists dates back to the Meiji era, but their postwar outreach was especially blessed, leading to the founding of many Baptist *Renmei* churches. Other smaller mission groups have been able to start churches in smaller towns around Kumamoto, Oita, and Miyazaki. Thankfully these churches are continuing on in spite of decreasing population.

27 The Kyushu district has more population per church than any other district in western Japan. The Saga prefecture is worst of all having only one church for over 30,000 people, and four others have less than one per 20,000. Some progress has been made in the last ten years, but this last year not one new church was started in Saga, Oita, or Miyazaki. Pray that at least one church be started in each of these three prefectures.

28 One of the unchurched cities, Taku in Saga prefecture, at last has a new church. Pray that the first Protestant churches may be started in Matsuura (Nagasaki) and Kaseda (Kagoshima). There are 358 villages and towns without churches, with eleven of these (five in Fukuoka) having a population of more than 20,000. Six are commuter towns with increasing populations.

The Protestant World in Japan

In Japan there are 7,726 Protestant churches (Church Information Service, 11/96), 1,037 Roman Catholic churches, and 75 Russian Orthodox churches (Christian Yearbook *Nenkan*, 1997). If somewhat questionable groups, excluding cults, were included, the total would be about 9,200. There are over 160 different Protestant denominations and church associations. The largest group is the Japan United Church of Christ (*Kyodan*) with 1,728. Two groups have over 300 churches and ten have over 100. These thirteen groups represent two thirds of all Protestants.

There are 3,118 churches in the Japan Council of Churches (NCC) with members including mainline denominations like the United Church of Christ, Episcopalians, Evangelical Lutherans, Baptist Renmei, Baptist Domei, the South Korean Church and others. Their evangelical counterpart with 1,428 churches, is the Japan Evangelical Association (JEA). A number of evangelical churches have yet to join JEA, and within the NCC there are also churches that can easily be called evangelical. So probably more than half of the Protestant churches in Japan can be called evangelical.

The NCC is part of the ecumenical World Council of Churches, which seeks to relate to the Roman Catholics and the Eastern Orthodox fellowships.

JEA is part of the World Evangelical Fellowship, and at the regional level the Evangelical Fellowship of Asia (EFA). The Lausanne International Committee is another evangelical worldwide network, but at present there is no recognized connection with the Evangelicals in Japan.

The multiplicity of denominations in Japan, nearly 170, seems a great shame in view of the Bible doctrine of the Church, and must be greatly confusing to seekers. But far from being an obstacle to God's blessing, such divisions have prevented the spread of liberal theology (by isolating one denomination from another), and secondly have resulted in the considerable increase in the number of churches throughout Japan, from just over 2,000 in 1950 to over 7,000 in 1996.

Hugh Trevor, retired OMF missionary
Japan's Post-War Protestant Churches, pg. 87

29 Pray for the ministry of Ochanomizu Christian Center in Tokyo. It was a burden for college student work that birthed the center right after the War. Now, besides the student outreach, it provides meeting rooms and office space for JEA, JEMA and many evangelical ministries.

30 Pray for the Japan Evangelical Missionary Association (JEMA) made up of 1,295 missionaries and 43 mission organizations. Pray for spiritual power and faith as they minister in many resistant situations.

31 Pray for the Japan Evangelical Association representing 1,428 churches, 52 church associations, and 37 para-church groups.

1 Church Information Service (CIS) each year sets this day as the time for the yearly tabulation of population, number of churches, membership, etc. Pray for CIS and their statistical analysis work, their ministry of referring people to evangelical churches, and their help for church planters in area analysis.

2 Pray for the Kansai Mission Research Center (KMRC) as it gathers and distributes data concerning mission work in Japan and the world, conducts seminars and publishes literature to assist the church in its mission.

3 Pray for the Japan Evangelical Theological Society as it does research and seeks to help the church grow strong in an evangelical understanding of the Word of God.

4 The Tokyo Mission Research Institute (TMRI) is dedicated to the research of important issues that hinder or stimulate the building of a solid Christian church in Japan. They sponsor study programs, research and publishing.

5 The weekly Christian Shinbun (newspaper) is dedicated to publishing world and Japan news which will strengthen the evangelical church and Christians. The other Christian newspaper, called the Christ Shinbun was begun before the War and primarily ministers to mainline churches. Pray that these papers will effectively encourage the believers.

福岡 **Fukuoka**

Capital: Fukuoka City
Population: 4,895,201
Cities: 23
  With 1 church: 5
Towns/Villages: 74
  With no churches: 49
  With 20,000 pop. &
   no churches: 5

Size: 4,961 km²
Density: 987 people/km²
Churches: P 273, C 37
Church per pop.: 1:17,931
Worship attendance: 9,317
Attendance/church: 34
Missionaries: 72

Geography

Fukuoka is located on the north side of Kyushu. Its northeastern section faces the Sea of Suo. On the north is the Sea of Hibiki, and the northwest the Sea of Genkai. The southeast borders Oita and Mt. Hiko, the south Kumamoto at the Chikuhi mountain range, and the southwest Saga at the Seburi mountain chain. The intricate Tsukushi mountain region surrounds the Tsukuba, Fukuoka and Nogata Plains. Other flat lands include some plains along the shoreline and small basins. The northern area has the typical climate found along the Sea of Japan, and the south enjoys the weather from the Inland Sea. As a whole, the climate is mild.

Industry & Economy

Even though agricultural production and the percentage of people engaged in agriculture are the smallest in Kyushu, the Chikugo Plain produces good yields of rice, barley, vegetables, and fruits. The forestry and fishing industries are about the national average. The Chikuho coal mines have helped the North Kyushu region become one of the nation's four major industrial districts. Despite the fact that there has been a decrease in the demand for coal, the economy of North Kyushu is still thriving because of the manufacturing industry.

Cultural Background

Some of the major ancient civilizations of Japan originated in Fukuoka. After the establishment of the Yamato Government, its local governmental agency was located here to maintain a direct connection with the main authority. Because of this historic background, the people of Fukuoka are sophisticated, openhearted, and less discriminatory against outsiders. Its closeness to the Asian mainland has brought many people to Fukuoka. It is presently home to 280,000 foreign people, more than any other prefecture in western Japan. One downside to this high number of outsiders is the fact that the population of Fukuoka is constantly fluctuating.

Religious Milieu

Many shrines with ancient traditions and festivals can be found in Fukuoka, like the Munakata, Miyajidake, Kashiigu, and Dazaifu Tenmangu Shrines. The number of famous Buddhist temples is very limited, but a large number of Buddhist followers reside here. The *Kirishitan* influence was felt early, but was not welcomed by the local lords and many people were martyred. When the ban on Christianity was lifted, the Catholic church first began its ministry by locating and identifying the hidden *Kirishitan*. A number of Protestant groups work in this area, led by the early ministry of the Japan Baptist Convention (*Renmei.*)

The Mission

On Kyushu Island, only Fukuoka and Kumamoto are experiencing population growth especially in their major cities. The number of churches per population is the highest on the island, and yet is well below the national average. An aggressive ministry is strongly needed, especially in the five towns where the population exceeds 20,000 people and there are no churches. That makes more than 130,000 people with no access to a church!

6 Pray for the Christian schools: Fukuoka Women's Jogakuin (college, jr high and high school, jr college), Seinan Gakuin (jr high and high school, college), Seinan Women's Jogakuin (jr and high school, jr college, college at Kita Kyushu), Orio Women's Joshi Gakuen (jr and high school at Kita Kyushu, Home Economy Jr College).

7 Pray for the Fukuoka Kameyama Eiko Hospital at Shime and also for the Christians employed at secular hospitals and clinics.

8 Pray for the Christian social services: Hisayama Ryoikuen, which has long been caring for the severely mentally and physically disabled, and Omuta Kciaicn and Keiai Work Center, providing placement services to the disabled. Pray for the salvation of the many foreign residents in Fukuoka.

9 Pray for the Fukuoka YMCA Hotel, and for the Christian book stores: Life Center at Fukuoka, Shinseikan at Fukuoka, Jordan Fukuoka Branch Store, and the Jordan Kita Kyushu Branch.

10 Pray that an evangelistic TV ministry be started, for *True Salvation* aired on Kyushu Asahi Radio. Pray for the Kyushu Gospel Association and Fukuoka Pastors' Fellowship.

Fukuoka is home to 280,000 foreigners in Japan. Read Psalm 63:1-3 and ask the Lord to make the church a blessing to these "strangers and exiles."

佐賀 Saga

Capital: Saga City
Population: 885,599
Cities: 7
  With 1 church: 3
Towns/Villages: 42
  With no churches: 36
  With 20,000 pop. &
  no churches: 1

Size: 2,433 km^2
Density: 364 people/km^2
Churches: P 29, C 11
Church per pop.: 1:30,538
Worship attendance: 650
Attendance/church: 22
Missionaries: 2

Geography

Saga is located in the northwestern part of Kyushu, facing the Sea of Ariake on the south and the Sea of Genkai on the north. It shares a border with Fukuoka on the east and Nagasaki on the west. The Islands of Iki and Tsushima, both of which belong to Saga, are located only 200 kilometers off the shoreline of South Korea. Saga has three main geographic features: the Seburi Mountain Chain in the north, hill countries in the west, and the Saga Plain in the south. The climate throughout Saga is relatively mild except for the mountainous regions and the area around the Sea of Genkai where an occasional winter front brings cold weather.

Industry & Economy

Saga's economy is solidly based on agriculture. In fact, rice grown on the Saga Plain was so successfully irrigated by its many canals that the prefecture once ranked as the nation's number one producer of rice. The more popular products of Saga include tangerines grown at the base of the mountains and seaweed from the Sea of Genkai. A well-known specialty of the district is Arita's traditional ceramic ware. The overall economy relies heavily on neighboring Fukuoka, the economic center of Kyushu, and it is unlikely that Saga will ever be economically independent. The few tourist sites include Yoshinogari, an ancient ruin, and some hot springs.

Cultural Background

People of Saga are known for their conservative nature. However, they are also known to be warmhearted, even having the nickname, "Saga, The Developer of Kind People." Many influences have shaped the culture here. Korea and China certainly brought their cultures in ancient days. The *Kirishitan* influence was felt throughout Kyushu. During the Edo period, Saga was ruled by various feudal clans including the Saga clan headed by Lord Nabeshima. This background has given them their conservative nature, as well as an openness to the new. The fact that one of the first baptized *Kirishitan* was from Saga provides an interesting symbol of this characteristic.

Religious Milieu

Traditional shrines found in Saga include the Yutoku Inari Shrine in Kashima, the Taku Shrine of Confucius in Taku, and the Matsubara Shrine where Lord Nabeshima of the Saga clan is worshiped. One of the newer religions, *"Taido* Preservation of Health" group, began here and is headquartered in the town of Fuji, north of Saga City. It grew quickly and started branches throughout the country. It has now run into a money scandal that has become a major social issue.

The Mission

When Wakasanokami Masanori Murata, the counselor of the Saga clan, was in Nagasaki as a navy officer, he came upon a Bible which had been retrieved from the ocean. Missionary Guido Verbeck later led him and his brother, Ayabe Murata, to faith and baptism. Over many years the samurai spirit has served as a spiritual support to the people of Saga. In the beginning of the Meiji era the first Lutheran Church in Japan was begun in Saga City. The examples of the Murata brothers and the first Lutheran Church, coupled with the samurai spirit of the area, should encourage us in prayer and vision for the area.

11 Pray for a strong spirit of cooperation among the pastors and believers of Saga's 27 churches.

12 Pray that more people listen to *The Light of The World* aired on NBC in Nagasaki and come to Christ. Pray that the churches of the prefecture hold rallies to promote the ministry.

13 Pray for the Christian social ministries of Zion's Garden, Megumi Garden, Fuji Gakuen, and that Christian schools and hospitals/clinics be started in this prefecture.

14 Pray that the 36 unchurched towns and villages soon have access to the gospel through local fellowships. Also, pray for the three cities with only one church.

15 Pray that the testimony of Christian pioneers and present-day Christian leaders from Saga be better known and serve as an encouragement for the gospel throughout the area.

Saga has the lowest percentage of churches per population, 1:30,538. Read Isaiah 41:15,16 and ask the Lord to make the small church in Saga a powerful tool for the harvest.

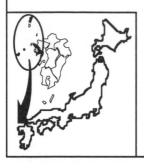

長崎 **Nagasaki**

Capital: Nagasaki City
Population: 1,550,220
Cities: 8
  With 0 churches: 1
  With 1 church: 1
Towns/Villages: 71
  With no churches: 59
  With 20,000 pop. & no churches: 1

Size: 4,112 km^2
Density: 377 people/km^2
Churches: P 61, C 130
Church per pop.: 1:25,413
Worship attendance: 1,265
Attendance/church: 21
Missionaries: 17

Geography

Nagasaki, with the exception of Okinawa, is the westernmost prefecture of the nation. Not only is the prefecture itself a peninsula, but it is also has numerous peninsulas such as Shimabara, Nagasaki, Nishi Sonogi, Kita Matsuura, and Higashi Matsuura. The rest of Nagasaki faces the East China Sea and the Tsushima Strait, both of which are dotted with many small islands. The two volcanic ranges of Mt. Tara and Mt. Unzen recently have shown volcanic activity. Other than these there are no mountain ranges of note, nor are there any significant plains. The Tsushima warm current brings warm weather and heavy rain.

Industry & Economy

Agriculture and fisheries are considered the leading industries of the Nagasaki prefecture. Agriculture is actually limited due to the complexity of the land formations. Paddy fields are sparse, and cultivated farm land is just enough to supply domestic demand. The only high-yielding products are white potatoes (second in the nation) and sweet potatoes. Rich fishing banks and excellent seaports bring in thriving business, making it the nation's second largest haul. Laurel and mackerel are especially famous. The coal mines on the Matsuura Peninsula dominated the coal industry along with Hokkaido and Kita Kyushu. Now that coal is less in demand, the area is in a fast decline. The core of the manufacturing industry is ship building and electronics. There is a handful of large companies, but most are small family businesses.

Cultural Background

Geographically Nagasaki is the closest prefecture to Korea and China. During the Edo era of isolation, it became the only port open to certain international ships. Many of the influences from China, Portugal, and the Netherlands can be seen throughout the prefecture. The people here say that they are not eager to meet strangers, perhaps an indication of how conservative and traditional the prefecture is.

Religious Milieu

Catholic priests first landed at Kagoshima and the work spread northward to Hirado in Nagasaki. This prefecture produced early *Kirishitan*, many of whom died as martyrs during the oppression. Many feel that the famous Battle of Amakusa was not as much a religious fight as it was a riot by the people who were suffering from heavy oppression.

However, because of the high profile of the Christians, one major result of the battle was their strong persecution. When the country opened during the Meiji era, many hidden *Kirishitan* were identified and churches were reestablished. While the number of Catholics is highest in the nation, Protestants are relatively few. Nagasaki has Kyushu's highest percentage of Buddhists.

The Mission

The example of how the *Kirishitan* survived over 300 years of oppression, maintaining a secret faith, is an amazing story. Also, the example of believers who endured the atomic bomb, committing themselves to God, and then mobilizing to promote world peace, is a testimony to the truth of God's Word. That Bible-based faith is still needed for each church in the prefecture.

16 Pray for the Christian schools: Kassui Gakuin (jr high and high school, women's jr college and college at Nagasaki) with a long Christian history; Chinzei Gakuin (high school and Nagasaki Wesleyan Jr College at Isahaya), Nagasaki Gakuin (Foreign Language Jr College), and others. Pray that these schools will be strongly based on the Bible.

17 There seems to be no Protestant medical facilities in the prefecture. Pray for the testimony of the Christian doctors and nurses working in secular facilities.

18 There are no known Christian social welfare facilities. Facilities for the elderly and disabled are much needed. Pray that the people suffering find the Light, and remember the Christians who are helping those who are suffering.

19 Pray for the Nagasaki Zion Christian Book Store. Pray that Christian camp and retreat facilities be established, and that a television ministry starts. Pray for *The Light of The World* aired on NBC Nagasaki Radio.

20 Pray that the first Protestant church will soon be started in Matsuura. Also pray for villages and towns with no churches. Pray for a strong sense of partnership among the pastors and churches.

Nagasaki prefecture is the home of some Christians who endured much suffering and oppression. Their faithfulness is a bold testimony to the grace of God. Read Revelation 2:3,10-11 and ask the Lord to grant new grace, strength and boldness to the believers here.

Crusade Evangelism

After Japan was defeated in the War, the victor nation, America, stepped in with a major relief effort including food necessary for survival. Western churches also gave Japan special attention with a number of evangelistic and church-help programs. The Pocket Testament League distributed Gospels of John throughout the country. Evangelistic meetings were also conducted in every prefecture. In the big cities like Tokyo large halls were rented for the preaching of the gospel. Crusade or mass evangelism started seriously around 1950, and in 1956 Billy Graham came for meetings at the Memorial Hall in Tokyo.

At the same time in the mainline churches Toyohiko Kagawa and Kiyomatsu Kimura, who had been active in evangelism before the War, conducted large evangelistic meetings. Stanley Jones and others from abroad also shared the message throughout the country. In 1950 the Lacour Music Ministry began a nationwide evangelism outreach that resulted in 33 new churches by 1967. In 1959 there was a large crusade in Osaka with Bob Pierce of World Vision. In 1961 a similar crusade was held in Tokyo. About that time Koji Honda was given a burden to preach the gospel in evangelistic meetings around Japan. He formed the Japan Gospel Crusade and conducted his first major crusade in Tokyo in 1964.

In 1967 the first Billy Graham Crusade was held in Tokyo. The second crusade in 1980 was held in Okinawa, Osaka, Fukuoka and Tokyo, with number three taking place at the Tokyo Dome in 1994. The previous fall, the All-Japan Koshien Revivial Mission with Rev. Takimoto took place in Kobe.

There have been many other major crusades centered around evangelists coming to Japan, but very few that have featured Japanese evangelists. The effectiveness of these large crusades is always debated. Certainly for Japan to come to Christ there must be an emphasis on local churches cooperating to reach their local areas. At the same time we must not neglect the larger national and global evangelistic perspective.

During the four-day Mission 94 Billy Graham Crusade 125,000 attended the Tokyo Dome meetings. An additional 21,222 viewed the crusade at 58 satellite locations. 53,500 went forward. 12,101 made decisions of some kind, of which 3,300 were first-time commitments to Christ. Pray for the many people who have made decisions at major crusades in the past, that they remember those decisions and faithfully follow Christ.

21 The Word of Life (*Inochi no Kotoba*) Evangelistic Association has 18 different ministries, all dedicated to evangelism through literature and radio/TV media.

22 Christian Literature Crusade (CLC) began in England and started its work in Japan right after the War. This ministry includes the publishing and distributing of evangelical literature through 12 different book stores throughout Japan.

23 The ministry of Every Home Crusade (EHC) began in Japan, and now has work in 90 different countries. Their mission is to touch whole nations through the distribution of evangelistic tracts to every home. In Japan they have placed literature in every home several times.

24 New Life League, now known as New Life Mission (*Shinsei Senkyodan*) is seeking to reach Japan and the world through the printing and distribution of Bibles and literature. It is the largest Christian printing company in Asia. Besides its important ministry in Japan, it has been printing large numbers of Bibles for Russia and China.

25 In our generation the most famous Japanese evangelist is Koji Honda (now in his 80s). Pray for his active ministry and for the organization which supports him, the Japan Gospel Crusade.

26 The Japan Christian Evangelistic Association (*Nihon Kirisuto Dendokai*) was formed with a vision to bring ten million people to Jesus. They assist local churches and evangelists to effectively present the gospel.

27 Pray for the various groups that are working in crusade evangelism and church growth: the Japan Christian Mission (*Nihon Dainamikku Kurusedo*), Japan Calvary Crusade, All Japan Revival Mission, All Japan Gospel Mission and others.

28 Pray for the Japan Evangelists Association (*Nihon Dendosha Kyoryokukai*). This group was formed in 1983 by some of those who attended the 1983 Itinerant Evangelists Congress in Amsterdam. They seek to encourage, train and send out traveling evangelists throughout the country.

November 29~December 3

熊本 Kumamoto

Capital: Kumamoto City
Population: 1,865,373
Cities: 11
  With 1 church: 2
Towns/Villages: 83
  With no churches: 67
  With 20,000 pop. &
   no churches: 1

Size: 7,215 km^2
Density: 259 people/km^2
Churches: P 87, C 17
Church per pop.: 1:21,441
Worship attendance: 2,467
Attendance/church: 28
Missionaries: 23

Geography

Kumamoto is located in the central area of Kyushu, touching Fukuoka, Oita, Miyazaki, and Kagoshima prefectures. The west faces the Sea of Ariake, Shimabara Bay, and the Sea of Yatsushiro. The Kyushu Mountain Chain, with the highest peaks on the island, runs through the southern region. In the north are the Tsukuhi mountains. The active volcano, Mt. Aso with its crater basin about 130 km. in circumference, is the largest of its kind in the world. The Udo Peninsula projects into the ocean where the Amakusa Islands are scattered. The area around Kumamoto City experiences drastic temperature variations, but the overall climate is mild and warm.

Industry & Economy

The people of Kumamoto are dependent on agriculture, livestock, and forest industries. Due to vast cultivated fields, agriculture is ranked seventh in the nation and second in Kyushu, following Kagoshima. A wide variety of crops including rice, barley, vegetables and fruits, is grown here. Kumamoto is the top producer of watermelons and other melons. It is the top producer of milk in Kyushu, with farms centering around Mt. Aso and Kumamoto City. Heavy industry includes chemical and paper/pulp. Regrettably, Minamata Disease was a by-product of the heavy industry and has caused nationwide attention as one of the country's biggest environmental problems.

Cultural Background

Generally speaking, the people of Kyushu are conservative and follow traditions; the people of Kumamoto are known to be even more so. They are noted for being genuine, single minded, liking an argument, conservative yet at times defiant. The largest percentage in the nation feel that Kumamoto is a good place to live.

Religious Milieu

Kumamoto people tend to be religiously oriented, and a large number identify themselves as Buddhists. The famous temples and shrines found here include the Aso Shrine predating the Nara era, and the Kikuchi and Kato Shrines, both dedicated to the worship of ancient warriors. Although the number of *Kirishitan* grew when the prefecture was ruled by Lord Yukinaga Konishi, his successor, Lord Kiyomasa Kato, suppressed Christianity. Many secret *Kirishitan* were believed to live in Amakusa. The Protestant ministry began when Captain L.L. Janes was asked to establish a school at Kumamoto. His Bible study classes at the school were especially effective.

The Mission

In 1876 at Mt. Hanaoka in the city of Kumamoto, ten students at the Kumamoto Western School signed a pledge of commitment under the leadership of Mr. Janes. The group became known as the Kumamoto Band. The Yokohama, Sapporo, and Kumamoto Bands are considered three main streams of Japanese Protestantism. Can we hope for new streams for Christ in our day?

29 Pray for Junshin Gakuen (Kumamoto Faith Girls' High School) with 100 years of history, and equally old Kyushu Gakuin (jr high and high school), and Kyushu Jogakuin Women's School (jr high, high school, and jr college). Pray that they will maintain a strong Bible-based education.

30 Pray for the Kikuchi Reimei Episcopal Church, providing care for those afflicted by Hansen's disease. Much spiritual support is needed even after recovery.

1 Pray for the Christian social service centers: Kumamoto Light House for the blind and Kumamoto Light House Nozomi Home for the mentally disabled. Also pray for Jiaien (Care House, etc.) for the elderly.

2 Pray for the Christian camp/retreat facilities: Kumamoto YMCA Aso Camp, Nishiyama Inn, both at Aso, and Lutheran Aso Mountain Villa at Choyo. Pray for the Kumamoto Christian Book Store.

3 Pray that evangelistic TV programs will soon be shown. Pray that *The Light of The World* aired on Kumamoto Radio be utilized to the fullest. Pray that pastors in the prefecture establish strong fellowship and cooperation through the Kumamoto Pastors' Association and other means.

Kumamoto prefecture gave birth to a group of dedicated Christians in the late 1800s that had a great impact on the Christian church. Read Judges 5:2 and ask the Lord for such days and such men again for the nation of Japan.

December 4~8

大分 Oita

Capital: Oita City
Population: 1,241,164
Cities: 11
  With 1 church: 3
Towns/Villages: 47
  With no churches: 39
  With 20,000 pop. &
  no churches: 0

Size: 6,338 km^2
Density: 196 people/km^2
Churches: P 62, C 16
Church per pop.: 1:20,019
Worship attendance: 1,516
Attendance/church: 24
Missionaries: 8

Geography

Oita is located in the northeast part of Kyushu. In the east the Bungo Channel separates it from Shikoku, and in the north is the Suo Sea and Yamaguchi Prefecture. Fukuoka is in the northwest, Kumamoto in the southwest, and Miyazaki in the south. In the south is part of the Kyushu Mountains. Ancient violent volcanic activity in the north created the scenic Yaba Kei Gorge and the Kunisaki Peninsula. In the tablelands of the south and east are the Kuju Mountains and Beppu Hot springs with scenic peaks in the background that still are active volcanos, like the Tsurumi Dake. The only real flat area is found at Oita and Nakatsu. Generally the weather is warm with much rain, but the Kunisaki Peninsula and the north receive little rain.

Industry & Economy

Industrial development has never taken off, so that even though the percentage of cultivated land is small, the prefecture remains agriculturally based. There are not really any special products, and neither livestock nor fishing is very productive. However, because of the large forest area centered in Hita in the west, Oita ranks first or second in lumber outside of Hokkaido and Tohoku. The prefecture is blessed with large mineral deposits. So even though industry has been slow to develop, manufacturing should have a bright future.

Cultural Background

Oita has a long history of tradition dating back into mythical times. Perhaps it is because of its location on the island that Oita has always tended to be different from the rest of Kyushu. The Kansai and Shikoku influence has been strong, giving the people a positive attitude, individualism and an emphasis on rationalism. Oita native, Yukichi Fukuzawa, the famous founder of Keio University, is a perfect example of the Oita spirit.

Religious Milieu

The Usa Shrine is one of the most famous ancient worship locations. Chusonji and Fukiji Temples along with many others mark the long religious background. Particularly from Usa through to the Kunisaki Peninsula magic and divination are evident. In the south around Usuki over 50 ancient stone statues of Buddha can be seen. Francis Xavier received the blessing of Lord Otomo in Oita in 1551 which led to many becoming *Kirishitan*. The oppressive anti-Christian policy of the Tokugawa government extended into the Meiji era, leaving prejudice and negativity, even after it was legal to become a Christian.

The Mission

Eager Protestant missionaries came to Oita in the early Meiji era as English teachers. They were able to establish the Oita Methodist church in 1888. It is recorded that the next year, at a New Year's Eve prayer meeting, the Holy Spirit brought a great revival to the church, and the young people went throughout the area evangelizing.

4 There do not appear to be any Christian schools in the prefecture. Let us join our hearts together for this need. Also pray for the Christian teachers that they might be as zealous as the Meiji era English teachers.

5 There is no indication of Christian medical facilities. Pray that if there are Christian medical workers that they can be joined together in fellowship and encouragement.

6 Remember the work of the Christian social ministries at the Eikoen, Beppu Heiwaen (Both are orphanages at Beppu), and for the special nursing home and day-care service, carried on by Izumi no Sono at Nakatsu.

7 Pray for the Christian book store service, Oita Life Center. Many areas of the prefecture do not have easy access to Christian literature. New effective methods of distribution are needed.

8 Pray that evangelistic TV programing becomes available. *Children of the Star* is broadcast on Oita Broadcasting. Also pray that there will be God-honoring fellowship among the churches and pastors.

Oita prefecture tasted revival in the late 1800s. Read Psalm 80:1-19 and ask the Lord to send revival fires to the church again.

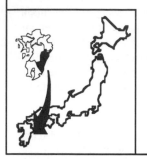

宮崎 Miyazaki

Capital: Miyazaki City
Population: 1,188,070
Cities: 9
 With 1 church: 2
Towns/Villages: 35
 With no churches: 27
 With 20,000 pop. &
  no churches: 2

Size: 7,198 km^2
Density: 165 people/km^2
Churches: P 63, C 15
Church per pop.: 1:18,858
Worship attendance: 1,177
Attendance/church: 19
Missionaries: 7

Geography

Miyazaki is located in the southeastern region of Kyushu. In the north is Oita at the Kyushu mountain range, in the west Kumamoto, and in the southwest Kagoshima at Mt. Kirishima and the neck of the Osumi Peninsula. On the east facing the Sea of Hyuga is a 100-kilometer stretch of monotonous shoreline. The distance from north to south is 170 kilometers, and from east to west is 70 kilometers. The Miyazaki Plain is located around the middle of the shoreline. Running through the plain is the Oyodo River whose upstream areas include the Miyakonojo and Kobayashi Basins. Weather is generally warm with heavy rainfall. There is never snow on the plains, but occasional torrential rains and typhoons during the rainy season can cause much damage.

Industry & Economy

The number of agricultural workers is decreasing, but they still make up over half of the labor force. Rice and barley are not very productive crops, but animal husbandry is quite strong. Volcanic ash covering the vast flat land areas and the rock structure hinder grain production. High yielding products include bell peppers (highest in the nation), white potatoes (third), Japanese radishes, and taro potatoes. The fishing industry does well in spite of its small fishing area. The heavy and manufacturing industries are underdeveloped due to geographical factors.

Cultural Background

More than 2,000 ancient burial mounds, and many ancient cultural relics have been unearthed in Miyazaki prefecture. Takachiho is the origin of the birth-myth of the nation. With this cultural background it is easy to see why the people of Miyazaki place high value on tradition and a sense of belonging to the community. This all-encompassing force in turn probably puts a thirst in many to be more positive and open to the outside.

Religious Milieu

An awareness survey reveals that the people have a strong interest in religious issues. There are many shrines with mythological backgrounds like Udo Shrine, Miyazaki Shrine and Takachiho Shrine. The acceptance of Christianity by the Otomo clan of Bungo sparked the spread of Catholicism, and it reached Hyuga where many became *Kirishitan*. Both Catholic and Protestant missionary efforts began at the end of the Meiji era. The Protestants started one year earlier than the Catholics, and were able to start churches in the major cities in just ten years.

The Mission

In Miyazaki, as well as each prefecture, our churches are blessed because of the sacrifices and labor of our Christian forerunners. Two towns (Mimata and Kunitomi) with growing populations of over 20,000 still do not have any churches. Is it possible for some of the 63 churches in this prefecture to take on the challenge to start a church in these towns? Let's claim a vision from God and reach out to the areas around us.

9 We desire to have at least one Christian school in each prefecture. Let's pray that the Miyazaki prefecture will soon have one. Pray that the Christian teachers and staff be effective witnesses to their students.

10 With no Christian medical facilities, let us pray that the Christian doctors and nurses provide their patients with not only physical but also spiritual healing and that they bear witness to their colleagues.

11 Christian social services can offer encouragement to the Christians as well as be an excellent instrument to spread the Christian faith. Pray that Christian welfare services be soon established in Miyazaki. Pray for the Christians working in the social services field.

12 Camping and retreat facilities are needed to help the church work here. Pray for the only Christian book store, Miyazaki Gospel Book Store, that the literature will strengthen Christians, and also provide an effective witness to the non-Christian.

13 Pray that a TV ministry be soon started. Pray for *The Light of The World* and *True Salvation* aired on Miyazaki Radio. Pray for a sense of unity and cooperation among the pastors and churches.

Miyazaki prefecture saw zealous church planting with rapid growth when missionaries first came to the prefecture. Read Nehemiah 4:6 and ask the Lord to grant such leadership, vision and determination to the church here.

145

December 14~18

鹿児島 Kagoshima

Capital: Kagoshima City
Population: 1,794,951
Cities: 14
  With no churches: 1
  With 1 church: 4
Towns/Villages: 82
  With no churches: 62
  With 20,000 pop. & no churches: 1

Size: 9,166 km²
Density: 196 people/km²
Churches: P 75, C 70
Church per pop.: 1:23,933
Worship attendance: 1,687
Attendance/church: 22
Missionaries: 14

Geography

Kagoshima is located in the southernmost area of Kyushu and consists of two sections, the area on the island itself and the many islands in the adjacent ocean called the Koshikijima Isles and Satsunan Islands. Kagoshima borders Miyazaki on the east and Kumamoto on the north, while it faces the Pacific Ocean in the south and the East China Sea in the west. The complex Kagoshima Bay has the Osumi Peninsula on the east and the Satsuma Peninsula with Sakura Island on the west. Kagoshima has many volcanoes, Mt. Kirishima, Mt. Sakurajima, and Mt. Kaimondake. The temperature is mild, precipitation is high, and the biggest natural enemy is typhoons. The mainland of Kagoshima experiences occasional snowfalls.

Industry & Economy

Kagoshima's gross agricultural product ranks as the best in western Japan and fourth in the nation. Satsuma (sweet potato) is the old nickname for the prefecture, which produces 30% of the nation's yield. Poultry and pigs are also important products. In forestry, the Yakushima cedar trees are considered the prefectural specialty. In the fishing industry it is top in the nation for the cultured yellowtail tuna and second for cultured eels. The manufacturing industry has not yet been developed.

Cultural Background

Kagoshima, along with Miyazaki, was one of the major ancient cultural centers on Kyushu Island. Due to its geographical isolation, its ancient cultural characteristics have been retained. They are traditional, conservative, and male dominant. They are known to be very emotional. They easily become zealous, but just as easily lose interest. After the Meiji Restoration closer ties with the central government were established. These ties helped to raise the educational standards to their present level.

146

Religious Milieu

The people of Kagoshima show an average interest in religion, but a fairly high percentage of people indicate a preference for a particular religion, with Buddhism and Shintoism getting about equal votes. Historic religious locations include the Kirishima Shrine and the Terukuni Shrine which enshrines the Lord of the Shimazu clan. Francis Xavier landed in Kagoshima in 1549 marking the beginning of Catholicism in Japan. Many became *Kirishitan*. However, many paid the sacrifice of martyrdom or were forced to recant of their faith during the years of severe oppression. Because of the Satsuma Rebellion, Protestant mission work had to wait until the end of the Meiji era, when a number of churches were started.

The Mission

The number of Protestant churches has increased from 56 to 75 in the past ten years, a 34% increase. At that rate there would be 100 churches within the decade. At the present, there is one church for every 24,000 people, but it could be one per 18,000 in ten years.

14 There seem to be no Protestant schools in Kagoshima. Pray that a Protestant school with solid Biblical roots be founded. Pray for the Christian teachers and personnel actually engaged in teaching.

15 Pray that Christian medical facilities become available as a witness to the gospel. Let's remember the Christian doctors, nurses, and other personnel as they seek to witness to colleagues and patients.

16 No Christian social welfare services are known in the whole prefecture. Needless to say, many people must be anxiously awaiting Christian involvement, especially services for the elderly. Pray for the Christians involved in caring for the underprivileged.

17 Pray for Christian Retreat Center in Tarumizu. Also pray for Kagoshima Hitomugi Book Store and Kanoya Christian Center Book Store, and for *True Salvation* aired on Minami Nippon Radio.

18 Pray for the Kagoshima Pastors' Fellowship, Kagoshima Christian Retreat, Kagoshima Evangelistic Cooperation Fellowship, and others. Kaseda City has no Protestant church. Pray that an evangelical church be started in addition to the existing Catholic church.

Kagoshima's church population has increased dramatically in the last ten years. Read Psalm 90: 16,17 and ask the Lord to bless the work of the church in even greater ways.

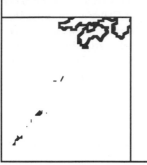

沖縄 Okinawa

Capital: Naha
Population: 1,287,023
Cities: 10
  With 1 church: 0
Towns/Villages: 43
  With no churches: 19
  With 20,000 pop. &
  no churches: 0

Size: 2,255 km^2
Density: 571 people/km^2
Churches: P 211, C 21
Church per pop.: 1:6,100
Worship attendance: 9,162
Attendance/church: 43
Missionaries: 96

Geography

Okinawa is the most southwestern prefecture of Japan. The Ryukyu Islands, a chain of more than 60 islands in the western Pacific Ocean, are part of Okinawa. The total land area is larger than Tokyo and the inhabitable land area is larger than Kyoto. Its slender shape measures 135 kilometers long and 4 - 28 kilometers wide. Okinawa Island is the largest and most important island of the Ryukyu Islands. Naha, the capital city, is on this island. The Ryukyus include the Okinawa Islands, and the Sakijima Islands consisting of Miyako, Yaeyama, and Senkaku. There are also single islands such as Kita Daito, Minami Daito, and Oki Daito. Okinawa has a tropical climate with little seasonal change. It is characterized by long summers, rapid weather changes, and typhoons.

Industry & Economy

Due to coral reefs and geographical isolation, along with vast U.S. military bases and other installations on the island, little land is left for farming. Thus the prefectural economy depends largely on U.S. military spending. The percentage of Okinawa's total revenue which comes from the service industry is the highest in the nation. The same is true for the percentage of people involved. Very little rice and few vegetables are grown, the main crops being pineapples and sugar cane.

Cultural Background

The people of Okinawa are racially and linguistically the same as the rest of Japan. However, the culture has developed differently because of isolation from the main islands. Taiwan, China, and the South Sea islands are close neighbors. Okinawa has suffered many historic tragedies. They were under dynasty control from the 12th century, then the isolation policy by the Edo government, dual control by the Satsuma clan and the Ming Dynasty of China, and the policies of the Meiji government. Governmental discrimination continued, followed by the fierce battles at the end of WW II, and the 27-year occupation by the US. Okinawa still carries scars from its past.

Religious Milieu

The result of a survey shows that 1.7% of the population are Buddhist believers and 0.3% Shintoists. Unlike other prefectures, traditional Buddhism and Shintoism are not rooted here. Instead, popular folklore beliefs based on ancestor worship are integral parts of the Okinawan's life. They include ceremonies and religious events with religious virgins called "Yuta" and "Noro" conducting incantations. These beliefs are closely related to "Monchu," a communal kinship society, which is a large obstacle to spreading the gospel.

The Mission

The first Protestant missionary here was Rev. Bettelheim who arrived in Naha Bay in May, 1846. His work included Bible translation. Okinawa became a foothold for the missionary work in the other islands. After the country became open to the outside, Okinawa ceased to be a needed stepping-stone, and was somewhat neglected. The occupation by the United States and presence of the US military became a blessing in disguise because it helped to spread the gospel here. The percentage of church members to population and Sunday worship attendance to the population are three times higher than the national average.

19 Pray for the Christian schools: Okinawa Christian Jr College at Nishihara, Okinawa Christian School International for the children of foreign residents at Yomitan, and Okinawa YMCA International Hotel Institute.

20 Pray for the Christian medical facilities: Olive Yama Hospital and affiliated Olive En for the elderly (both in Naha). Pray for Airaku En where Pastor Yasujiro Aoki devoted his life to those suffering from Hansen's disease before he himself was afflicted and died.

21 Pray for Christian welfare facilities: Airin'en for children, Ainosono for the disabled (both at Yonabaru), and Aino Mura for the elderly at Nakagusuku. Pray that they may give strong support and bring many to Christ.

22 Pray for the Christian camp/retreat centers: Okinawa Ginowan Seminar House and Pension Ecclesia at Ishigaki. Pray for the Life Center Naha Book Store and Okinawa Christian Book Store.

23 Pray for the Christian broadcasts: *Harvest Time* televised on Okinawa Television, and *The Light of The World*, *Children of The Star*, *True Salvation*, and *Baptist Hour*, aired on Okinawa Radio. Pray for a strong sense of cooperation, especially as the churches prepare for the JEA Congress on Evangelism in 2000.

Okinawa has the lowest percentage of Shinto/Buddhist believers in Japan. Read Acts 4:24-31 and ask the Lord to make the church bold in its testimony to the truth of the Gospel in this environment.

Christmas and the New Year

No other time of the year more perfectly spotlights the Japanese religious heart than the end of December and the first of January! The department stores and the small shops all start their Christmas advertisements and sales even before Advent. In November the younger children celebrate *Shichi-Go-San* (7-5-3) Day at the Shinto Shrine. It is a time when girls who are ages three or seven, and boys who are five, dress up in kimono and go to the shrine to receive a blessing.

Next comes Santa Claus. The gift-giving custom is usually limited to parents giving their children presents. The Christmas cake, to be eaten on Christmas Eve, has become a popular family experience. As soon as Christmas ends, parents prepare little envelopes of money to give their own children and those of relatives and friends as a New Year's gift. Often children will receive several hundred dollars. The Christmas decorations are replaced by the Shinto New Year's symbol, a pine branch attached to the front gate of each home.

Japanese who happen to be in the USA during this time are surprised to see Christmas trees still in place at New Year's time. Most Japanese head for temples or shrines early on New Year's Day to pray for safety and blessings for the new year. As they approach the front area, they toss a coin into the offering "trough," clap their hands, and pray.

To whom they pray is not important. The prayer may go to Buddha, an ancestor god, or one of the million Shinto gods. It doesn't really matter. The same thing can be seen in many homes which may still have a Buddhist family altar and also a Shinto god-shelf.

When Buddhism came to Japan, the Buddhist guardian spirits quickly took their place with the Shinto gods. Even the Indian Hindu gods became part of this spectrum of deities.

For the Japanese, syncretism is a very common reality, a part of daily life. In the midst of this, how do we effectively proclaim the gospel? Perhaps at times Japanese Christians have just added one more Big God to the others. The Christian work in Japan must present Jesus as the one and only Lord of all.

Christmas is the most effective time of the year to share the gospel in Japan. Throughout the country churches are cooperating in special concerts (The Messiah is one of the most popular), city-wide evangelistic meetings, and candle services. Most likely there are more than twice as many people who hear the gospel during this time than the total national Sunday morning attendance. Please pray for this extraordinary evangelistic season. From JEA Japan Update, *Fall, 1996.*